Table of Contents

Chapter 1

Chapter 2

Chapter 3

Chapter 4

Chapter 5

Chapter 8

Chapter 9

Chapter 10

Chapter 13

Chapter 14

Chapter 15

Chapter 16

Chapter 17

Chapter 18

Chapter 19

Chapter 20

Foreword

It was never my idea to publish a book when this study began. It simply began as a pastor trying to do the will of God by proclaiming the "whole counsel of God." I can only hope that the thousands of hours that were spent in preparing this study guide can and will be put to use by those who love and teach the Bible.

Many books are available today that specialize in prophecy. Some are verse-by-verse studies, while the majority are interpretations of prophetic events. I did not attempt to interpret the Word of God in twenty-first century terms. Rather, the following basic principles of Biblical interpretation have been followed in this study guide:

1. Never take a verse out of context to make a pretext.
2. Always compare Scripture with Scripture.
3. Never read into Scripture where Scripture is silent.
4. When Scripture is silent, consider the silence good.
5. Seek no other sense than the literal sense when the literal sense makes sense—lest it become nonsense.
6. Determine doctrines on Scripture rather than personal experience.
7. Allow Scripture to interpret itself.

By adhering to the above principles, the reader will find that this study guide will present only that which adheres to Scriptural teaching. The doctrine of eschatology has been so misunderstood in these last times. Many Christians are taught fables for facts and very little that is taught in many modern pulpits has anything to do with the Scriptures. Sadly, the greatest mistake in the church today is the lack of any Bible teaching regarding the Book of Revelation—a revealing of Jesus Christ.

As introduction to the study guide contents of this book, the author would ask the reader to keep the following in mind regarding prophecy and prophetical events:

What is Prophecy?

Prophecy is the presentation of future history as past events.

How is Prophecy Used?

Prophecy is used to relay God's messages of judgment or promise to man.

When is Prophecy Used?

Prophecy is used when God wishes to reveal future events so that:

1. Man may prepare for that event
2. He may prove His authority
3. He may give credence to His Word.

Who is Involved in Prophecy?

Prophecy involves:

1. God, as the Source of the Message
2. Prophet, as the Bearer of the Message
3. People, as the Receiver of the Message

Who is a True Prophet?

A True Prophet must meet the following guidelines:

1. He must receive his message from God
2. Every word of his prophecy must either be fulfilled or awaiting fulfillment
3. He can never be wrong in any specifics (e.g. dates, times, places, persons, event order, etc.)

Why Does God Use Prophecy?

God uses prophecy for the following reasons:

1. To reveal His omniscience to man
2. To communicate between an immortal God and mortal man
3. To allow man to have proof of His sovereignty

God promises a special blessing to those who "readeth, and they that hear the words of this prophecy, and keep those things which are written therein: for the time is at hand." May God richly bless you, the reader, as you study God's Word. May this study guide be only an aid to that study.

Acknowledgments

A very special acknowledgment to "Julie", a new convert who wanted to know when her pastor would teach on the Book of Revelation like all the preachers on the radio. After making light of her question, God used it to convict me of the need to do just that. When I first started the series that eventually became this book, I started out by saying that I was definitely not an authority, but that I could not get past the convicting words of a new believer, whose only desire was the knowledge of God's Word. Thank you, Julie, for letting God use your words to convict this preacher's heart.

I must thank all those men that I have called pastor. Each of them has added to my knowledge of the Bible in their own unique ways. First, I would like to thank John Taylor—pastor emeritus of New Testament Baptist Church. Thank you for building the strong foundation. Second, I would like to thank the ministry of Dr. Lee Roberson—pastor emeritus of Highland Park Baptist Church. Thank you for being my college pastor at Tennessee Temple. Third, I would like to thank Bro. George Trask—director of Sand Mountain Bible Camp Ministries. Thank you for an example of a righteous life. Fourth, I would like to thank Bro. James Waymire—founding pastor of Arnold Baptist Tabernacle. Thank you for being a encouraging friend. Fifth, I would like to thank Bro. Larry Stark—former pastor of Arnold Baptist Tabernacle. Thank you for lighting the fire in my life once again. Sixth, I would like to mention the late Dr. Jack Hyles—pastor of First Baptist Church. Thank you for teaching me so much about people and how to love them.

One last special word of thanks—first, to my family (who allowed me the thousands of hours necessary to finish this project) and lastly, to the members of Perry County Baptist Church (who permitted their pastor to try out this material on them—I love you all!) May God richly bless you as the "time is at hand."

Chapter 1

1 ¶ The Revelation of Jesus Christ, which God gave unto him, to shew unto his servants things which must shortly come to pass; and he sent and signified *it* by his angel unto his servant John:

2 Who bare record of the word of God, and of the testimony of Jesus Christ, and of all things that he saw.

3 ¶ Blessed *is* he that readeth, and they that hear the words of this prophecy, and keep those things which are written therein: for the time *is* at hand.

4 John to the seven churches which are in Asia: Grace *be* unto you, and peace, from him which is, and which was, and which is to come; and from the seven Spirits which are before his throne;

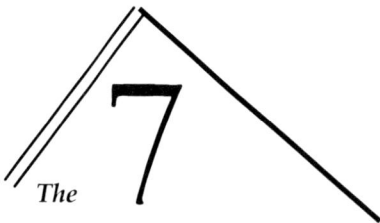

The 7

Churches

The Personal Foreword of the Book
Rev. 1:1-3

I. The Personality of the Revelation (1:1)
    A. Its Person—Jesus Christ
    B. Its Power—given by God to Him
II. The Purpose of the Revelation (1:1)—to make manifest future prophetic occurrences
    A. In Their Perfect Timing
    B. In His Promised Fulfillment
III. The Pattern of the Revelation (1:1-2)
    A. Signified by Angels
    B. Sent to John
        1. Because of his knowledge of the Scripture
        2. Because of his knowledge of the Saviour
        3. Because of his knowledge of the Subject
IV. The Promise of the Revelation (1:3)
    A. To those that read this book
    B. To those that hear this book
    C. To those that keep this book

The Formal Introduction to the Book
Rev. 1:4-11

I. The Formal Address of the Book
    A. To the Seven Churches in Asia (1:4,11)
        1. Ephesus
        2. Smyrna
        3. Pergamos
        4. Thyatira
        5. Sardis
        6. Philadelphia
        7. Laodicea

5 And from Jesus Christ, *who is* the faithful witness, *and* the first begotten of the dead, and the prince of the kings of the earth. Unto him that loved us, and washed us from our sins in his own blood,

6 And hath made us kings and priests unto God and his Father; to him *be* glory and dominion for ever and ever. Amen.

7 Behold, he cometh with clouds; and every eye shall see him, and they *also* which pierced him: and all kindreds of the earth shall wail because of him. Even so, Amen.

8 I am Alpha and Omega, the beginning and the ending, saith the Lord, which is, and which was, and which is to come, the Almighty.

ΑΩ

"I am Alpha and Omega, the beginning and the ending"

II. From The Trinity (1: 4-5)
    A. The Everlasting Father
        1. He Which Is
        2. Which Was
        3. Is to Come
    B. The Ever-Present Holy Spirit
        1. Complete in Purpose
        2. Controlled in Presence
    C. The Eternal Son…The Faithful Witness
        1. The First-Begotten of the Dead
        2. The Prince of the Kings of the Earth

III. The Deserved Adoration of the Book
    A. The Reasons for Adoration (1: 5-6)
        1. His Ransom—He First Loved Us
        2. Our Redemption—He Washed our Sins in His Blood
        3. Our Reward—His Heritage to Us
            a) He has made us Rulers—Kings
            b) He has made us Righteous—Priests
        4. His Right—His Due from Us
            a) Be glory—Praise
            b) And dominion—Power (Authority)
            c) Forever and Ever—Potency (Duration)
    B. The Results of Adoration (1:7)
        1. He shall come again in glory—The Second Advent of the Second Coming
        2. There shall be mixed reactions
            a) To the lost—wailing for impending judgment
            b) To the saved—waiting for impending Kingship

IV. The Divine Authorship of the Book (1: 8)
    A. His Name—Alpha and Omega

9 ¶ I John, who also am your brother, and companion in tribulation, and in the kingdom and patience of Jesus Christ, was in the isle that is called Patmos, for the word of God, and for the testimony of Jesus Christ.

10 I was in the Spirit on the Lord's day, and heard behind me a great voice, as of a trumpet,

11 Saying, I am Alpha and Omega, the first and the last: and, What thou seest, write in a book, and send *it* unto the seven churches which are in Asia; unto Ephesus, and unto Smyrna, and unto Pergamos, and unto Thyatira, and unto Sardis, and unto Philadelphia, and unto Laodicea.

12 And I turned to see the voice that spake with me. And being turned, I saw seven golden candlesticks;

13 And in the midst of the seven candlesticks *one* like unto the Son of man, clothed with a garment down to the foot, and girt about the paps with a golden girdle.

14 His head and *his* hairs *were* white like wool, as white as

"What thou seest, write in a book, and send *it* unto the seven churches which are in Asia; unto Ephesus, and unto Smyrna, and unto Pergamos, and unto Thyatira, and unto Sardis, and unto Philadelphia, and unto Laodicea."

B. His Nature—Co-equal and co-eternal with God

C. His Notability—Almighty Authority

V. The Human Penmanship of the Book—John the Beloved (1: 9)

    A. A Fellow Sufferer

    B. A Felon in the Land—exiled to Patmos for:

      1. The Word of God

      2. The Testimony regarding Jesus Christ

    C. A Foreseer of Future Events

      1. Through the Power of the Holy Spirit

      2. In the Place of God's Preparation—His Will

The Vision of the Seven Golden Candlesticks
Rev. 1: 10-20

I. The Meaning of the Seven Candlesticks—the Seven Churches (1: 10-12)

II. The Midst of the Seven Candlesticks—the Son of Man (Jesus)

    A. The Man Himself (1: 13-15)

      1. His Garment—a Robe (Righteousness)

      2. His Girdle—a Belt or Sash of Gold (Deity)

      3. His Head and Hair—White as Snow (Purity)

      4. His Gaze—Eyes of Fire (Judgment)

      5. His Feet—Fine Brass, tried in the Fire (Strong Judgment)

      6. His Voice—Sound of Many Waters (Authority)

    B. The Man's Manner (1:16)

      1. In His Right Hand—Seven Stars, Pastors of the seven churches (see 1:20)

snow; and his eyes *were* as a flame of fire;

15 And his feet like unto fine brass, as if they burned in a furnace; and his voice as the sound of many waters.

16 And he had in his right hand seven stars: and out of his mouth went a sharp twoedged sword: and his countenance *was* as the sun shineth in his strength.

17 And when I saw him, I fell at his feet as dead. And he laid his right hand upon me, saying unto me, Fear not; I am the first and the last:

18 I *am* he that liveth, and was dead; and, behold, I am alive for evermore, Amen; and have the keys of hell and of death.

19 Write the things which thou hast seen, and the things which are, and the things which shall be hereafter;

20 The mystery of the seven stars which thou sawest in my right hand, and the seven golden candlesticks. The seven stars are the angels of the seven churches: and the seven candlesticks which thou sawest are the seven churches.

"Write the things which thou hast seen, and the things which are, and the things which shall be hereafter"

2. Out of His Mouth—A Two-edged Sword, the Bible
3. His Countenance—Bright as the Sun
   a) His Fullness of Glory
   b) His Omnipotence
   c) His Deity
C. The Man's Message (1: 18-20)
   1. His Authority—Himself as:
      a) Eternal God
      b) Everlasting Conqueror
         (1) Over Death
         (2) Over the Grave
         (3) Over Hell
   2. His Aim—To Show:
      a) That which is Past—that which John had seen
      b) That which is Present—that which existed in John's present time
      c) That which is Future—that which shall be after John's time
   3. His Arrangement—To reveal His Word by His Word (1:20)
      a) Seven Stars—Seven Pastors
      b) Seven Golden Candlesticks—Seven Churches

The first chapter of the Book of Revelation introduced us to the Person of Jesus Christ, the authority of the prophecy as revealed to John, and the general outline of the rest of the book: 1) the things which were, 2) the things which are, and 3) the things which shall be hereafter. The next two chapters deal with the middle part of the general outline— the things which are. These churches are typical of

Chapter 2

1 ¶ Unto the angel of the church of Ephesus write; These things saith he that holdeth the seven stars in his right hand, who walketh in the midst of the seven golden candlesticks;

2 I know thy works, and thy labour, and thy patience, and how thou canst not bear them which are evil: and thou hast tried them which say they are apostles, and are not, and hast found them liars:

3 And hast borne, and hast patience, and for my name's sake hast laboured, and hast not fainted.

4 Nevertheless I have *somewhat* against thee, because thou hast left thy first love.

5 Remember therefore from whence thou art fallen, and repent, and do the first works; or else I will come unto thee quickly, and will remove thy candlestick out of his place, except thou repent.

6 But this thou hast, that thou hatest the deeds of the Nicolaitans, which I also hate.

7 He that hath an ear, let him

"Remember therefore from whence thou art fallen, and repent, and do the first works; or else I will come unto thee quickly, and will remove thy candlestick out of his place, except thou repent."

churches throughout history and of historical church eras, as well.

The Seven Churches
Rev. 2:1-3:22

I. Ephesus—The Church That Had Left Its First Love (2:1-7)
    A. Christ's Introduction to the Church
        1. Holds the Seven Stars--Authority
        2. Walks in the Midst of the Seven Candle-sticks—Association
    B. The Good That They Had Done
        1. Good Works
        2. Hard Labors
        3. Patience—Endurance under Trial
        4. Sound in Doctrine
        5. Hatred of Liberalism—Nicolaitans
            a) Moral Impurity—Liberty turned to License
            b) Separation of Classes—Clergy and Laity
    C. The Evil Which They Had Done
        1. They Had Moved Away From Christ's Priorities
        2. They Had Left, Not Lost Their First Love
    D. The Opportunity for Restoration
        1. Remember—from where you have fallen
        2. Repent—of your present condition
        3. Return—to the First Love that was left
    E. The Opportunity for Judgment
        1. Expeditious—He will come quickly
        2. Extreme—Removal of the candle-stick…

hear what the Spirit saith unto the churches; To him that overcometh will I give to eat of the tree of life, which is in the midst of the paradise of God.

8 ¶ And unto the angel of the church in Smyrna write; These things saith the first and the last, which was dead, and is alive;

9 I know thy works, and tribulation, and poverty, (but thou art rich) and *I know* the blasphemy of them which say they are Jews, and are not, but *are* the synagogue of Satan.

10 Fear none of those things which thou shalt suffer: behold, the devil shall cast *some* of you into prison, that ye may be tried; and ye shall have tribulation ten days: be thou faithful unto death, and I will give thee a crown of life.

11 He that hath an ear, let him hear what the Spirit saith unto the churches; He that overcometh shall not be hurt of the second death.

12 ¶ And to the angel of the church in Pergamos write; These things saith he which

THE MARTYRDOM OF POLYCARP

As told by John Foxe

"Polycarp, the venerable bishop of Smyrna, hearing that persons were seeking for him, escaped, but was discovered by a child. After feasting the guards who apprehended him, he desired an hour in prayer, which being allowed, he prayed with such fervency, that his guards repented that they had been instrumental in taking him. He was, however, carried before the proconsul, condemned, and burnt in the market place.

The proconsul then urged him, saying, "Swear, and I will release thee; reproach Christ."

Polycarp answered, "Eighty and six years have I served him, and he never once wronged me; how then shall I blaspheme my King, Who hath saved me?" At the stake to which he was only tied, but not nailed as usual, as he assured them he should stand immovable, the flames, on their kindling the fagots, encircled his body, like an arch, without touching him; and the executioner, on seeing this, was ordered to pierce him with a sword, when so great a quantity of blood flowed out as extinguished the fire. But his body, at the instigation of the enemies of the Gospel, especially Jews, was ordered to be consumed in the pile, and the request of his friends, who wished to give it Christian burial, rejected. They nevertheless collected his bones and as much of his remains as possible, and caused them to be decently interred."

the church
   F. The Promise to the Church
      1. Overcoming—Eat of the Tree of Life
      2. Overcoming—Eternity in Heaven

Smyrna was the church that was headed by the martyr Polycarp, a disciple of John's in the second century. It was one of only two churches addressed in a completely positive manner.

II. Smyrna—The Faithful, Persecuted Church (2: 8-11)
   A. Christ's Introduction to the Church
      1. The First and the Last—Eternality
      2. The Dead and Alive—Immortality
   B. Christ's Commendation to the Church
      1. Their Unapparent Wealth
      2. Their Apparent Witness
   C. Christ's Command to the Church
      1. Fear Not in Persecution
      2. Faithfulness in Persecution
   D. Christ's Promise to the Church
      1. Overcoming in Persecution—A Crown of Life
      2. Overcoming in Salvation—A Cure for the Second Death
III. Pergamos, The Church That Dwelled in Satan's Seat (2: 12-17)
   A. Christ's Introduction to the Church
      1. The Sharp Sword—The Powerful Word of God
      2. Two Edges—The Potent Judgment of God
   B. Christ's Praise for the Church
      1. Surviving in Satan's Seat—Health

hath the sharp sword with two edges;

13 I know thy works, and where thou dwellest, *even* where Satan's seat *is*: and thou holdest fast my name, and hast not denied my faith, even in those days wherein Antipas *was* my faithful martyr, who was slain among you, where Satan dwelleth.

14 But I have a few things against thee, because thou hast there them that hold the doctrine of Balaam, who taught Balac to cast a stumblingblock before the children of Israel, to eat things sacrificed unto idols, and to commit fornication.

15 So hast thou also them that hold the doctrine of the Nicolaitans, which thing I hate.

16 Repent; or else I will come unto thee quickly, and will fight against them with the sword of my mouth.

17 He that hath an ear, let him hear what the Spirit saith unto the churches; To him that overcometh will I give to eat of the hidden manna, and will give him a white stone, and in the stone a

The Doctrine of the Nicolaitans

- νικαω—nikao, to conquer

- λαος—laos, the people

This word means, literally "to conquer the people"—a division of the clergy and the laity.

This leads to:

1. The unimportance of Scripture
2. Totalitarianism in the pulpit
3. Oppression of the people
4. A blatant disregard for God's established order of authority
5. Abuse in financial matters
6. Different levels of expectation in living for the clergy and the laity
7. The destruction of the faith of the people by destroying sound doctrine.

2. Holding Fast His Name—Stamina
3. Not Denying His Faith—Loyalty
C.   Christ's Problem with the Church
    1. Doctrine of Balaam
      a) Compromise with the World
      b) Confusion before the Church
    2. Doctrine of the Nicolaitans
      a) "Destroyer of the People"
      b) Division of the People
D.   Christ's Proposal to the Church
    1. Repent
    2. Or else
      a) Sudden Judgment
      b) Sword of His Mouth—Righteous Judgment
E.   Christ's Promise to the Church
    1. Overcoming—Eating of the Hidden Manna
    2. Overcoming—Earning a White Stone
      a) New Name Written Thereon
      b) No Man Knows but He Who Receives It

A New Name

name written, which no man knoweth saving he that receiveth *it*.

18 ¶ And unto the angel of the church in Thyatira write; These things saith the Son of God, who hath his eyes like unto a flame of fire, and his feet *are* like fine brass;

19 I know thy works, and charity, and service, and faith, and thy patience, and thy works; and the last *to be* more than the first.

20 Notwithstanding I have a few things against thee, because thou sufferest that woman Jezebel, which calleth herself a prophetess, to teach and to seduce my servants to commit fornication, and to eat things sacrificed unto idols.

21 And I gave her space to repent of her fornication; and she repented not.

22 Behold, I will cast her into a bed, and them that commit adultery with her into great tribulation, except they repent of their deeds.

23 And I will kill her children with death; and all the churches shall know that I am he which searcheth the

JEZEBEL

Thyatira was a flourishing commercial city in Lydia, now part of modern Turkey.

IV.   Thyatira, The Church of Jezebel (2: 18-29)
     A.   Christ's Introduction to the Church
         1. Son of God—Deity
         2. Eyes Like a Flame of Fire—Devouring Judgment
         3. Feet Like Brass—Finishing Judgment
     B.   Christ's Praise for the Church
         1. Works for Christ—Initial
           a) Charity—Love for God
           b) Service—Love for Others
           c) Faith
           d) Patience
         2. Works for Christ—Latter
           a) More Abundant than the First— Plenty in Trials
           b) More Admirable than the First—Purity in Trials
     C.   Christ's Problem with the Church—the Doctrine of Jezebel
         1. Refusing to Teach Sound Doctrine
           a) Seduced the People—Subtlety of Deceit
           b) Spiritual Fornication—Separation Rejected
           c) Subtle, Questionable Practices Embraced—Sin Made Appealing
         2. Refusing to Repent at Christ's Command
           a) Desertion, Spiritual Ichabod—Apostasy even Through The Great Tribulation
           b) Death—Spiritual Progeny who Teach

reins and hearts: and I will give unto every one of you according to your works.

24 But unto you I say, and unto the rest in Thyatira, as many as have not this doctrine, and which have not known the depths of Satan, as they speak; I will put upon you none other burden.

25 But that which ye have *already* hold fast till I come.

26 And he that overcometh, and keepeth my works unto the end, to him will I give power over the nations:

27 And he shall rule them with a rod of iron; as the vessels of a potter shall they be broken to shivers: even as I received of my Father.

28 And I will give him the morning star.

29 He that hath an ear, let him hear what the Spirit saith unto the churches.

Chapter 3

1 ¶ And unto the angel of the church in Sardis write; These things saith he that hath the seven Spirits of God, and the seven stars; I know thy works, that thou hast a name

"I will give him the morning star."

and Practice the Same

        c) Deserving—Judgment that meets the Fervor of their Works

D.   Christ's Proposal to the Church

    1. To Those That Have Not the Doctrine of Jezebel—Hold Fast

    2. To Those That Have Not Known the Depths of Satan—Continue On

E.   Christ's Promise to the Church

    1. Overcometh—Power Over the Nations, A Place of Responsibility

    2. Overcometh—Ruled Over with a Rod of Iron—A Place of Security

    3. Overcometh—Given a Morning Star, A Sign of His Presence

The Church at Sardis was the church that had just about died. While not completely dead to the cause of Christ, there were a faithful few among the many, who were dead spiritually, that had not yet succumbed to the spiritual death all around them. Christ will have both commendation and criticism of this church.

V.   Sardis, The Living Dead Church (3: 1-6)

    A.   Christ's Introduction to the Church

        1. He That Hath the Seven Spirits—The Fullness of the Spirit

        2. He That Hath the Seven Stars—The Fullness of Authority

    B.   Christ's Analysis of the Church

        1. Has a Name of Living—Profession without Possession

        2. Art Dead—Reality versus Perception

that thou livest, and art dead.

2 Be watchful, and strengthen the things which remain, that are ready to die: for I have not found thy works perfect before God.

3 Remember therefore how thou hast received and heard, and hold fast, and repent. If therefore thou shalt not watch, I will come on thee as a thief, and thou shalt not know what hour I will come upon thee.

4 Thou hast a few names even in Sardis which have not defiled their garments; and they shall walk with me in white: for they are worthy.

5 He that overcometh, the same shall be clothed in white raiment; and I will not blot out his name out of the book of life, but I will confess his name before my Father, and before his angels.

6 He that hath an ear, let him hear what the Spirit saith unto the churches.

7 ¶ And to the angel of the church in Philadelphia write; These things saith he that is holy, he that is true, he that hath the key of David, he

Strengthen the things that remain:

1. *The Foundations*

2. *The Structure*

Fan the Embers:

1. *Of Passion—the heart of the church,* **Desire**

2. *Of Purpose—the soul of the church,* **Duty**

3. *Of Precepts—the lifeblood of the Church,* **Doctrine**

Remember Teaching

1. *Be Faithful in Attendance*

2. *Be Faithful in Observance*

3. *Be Faithful in Continuance*

Hold Fast—*τηρεω, *Cling to and Guard

1. *With Fervency*

2. *With Knowledge*

3. *With Compassion*

Return and Repent

1. *To Sound Doctrine*

2. *To Certain Truth*

C. Christ's Advice to the Church
   1. Stay Alert—Be Watchful
   2. Strengthen the Things Which Remain
   3. Study that which was First Received
   4. Stay Close to Him—Repent
D. Christ's Admiration for the Church—The Faithful Few
   1. Will Walk in White
   2. Worthy to do so
E. Christ's Announcement to the Church
   1. Overcometh—Clothed in White Raiment, Righteousness
   2. Overcometh—Careful to not blot out their name out of the Book of Life, Security
   3. Overcometh—Confession of their name before the Father and the Angels, Promise

VI. Philadelphia, the Church of Brotherly Love (3:7-12)
A. Christ's Introduction to the Church
   1. He That is Holy—Attribute of Christ, His Personality
   2. He That is True—Absoluteness of Christ, His Person
   3. He That Hath the Key of David—Authority of Christ, His Power
B. Christ's Praise for the Church
   1. The Open Door of the Gospel—Their Cause
   2. The Little Strength—Their Capacity
   3. Kept His Word—Their Carefulness
   4. Not Denied His Name—Their Constancy
C. Christ's Preservation of the Church
   1. Cause their Enemies to Worship before their feet

that openeth, and no man shutteth; and shutteth, and no man openeth;

8 I know thy works: behold, I have set before thee an open door, and no man can shut it: for thou hast a little strength, and hast kept my word, and hast not denied my name.

9 Behold, I will make them of the synagogue of Satan, which say they are Jews, and are not, but do lie; behold, I will make them to come and worship before thy feet, and to know that I have loved thee.

10 Because thou hast kept the word of my patience, I also will keep thee from the hour of temptation, which shall come upon all the world, to try them that dwell upon the earth.

11 Behold, I come quickly: hold that fast which thou hast, that no man take thy crown.

12 Him that overcometh will I make a pillar in the temple of my God, and he shall go no more out: and I will write upon him the name of my God, and the name of the city of my God, *which is* new Jerusalem, which cometh

Crowns in the Bible

Crown of Life
Jas 1:12 Blessed *is* the man that endureth temptation: for when he is tried, he shall receive the crown of life, which the Lord hath promised to them that love him.

Crown of Righteousness
2Ti 4:8 Henceforth there is laid up for me a crown of righteousness, which the Lord, the righteous judge, shall give me at that day: and not to me only, but unto all them also that love his appearing.

Soul-Winner's Crown
1Th 2:19 For what *is* our hope, or joy, or crown of rejoicing? *Are* not even ye in the presence of our Lord Jesus Christ at his coming?
Php 4:1 ¶ Therefore, my brethren dearly beloved and longed for, my joy and crown, so stand fast in the Lord, *my* dearly beloved.

Sufferer's or Crown of Persecution
Re 2:10 Fear none of those things which thou shalt suffer: behold, the devil shall cast *some* of you into prison, that ye may be tried; and ye shall have tribulation ten days: be thou faithful unto death, and I will give thee a crown of life.

Crown of Glory
1Pe 5:4 And when the chief Shepherd shall appear, ye shall receive a crown of glory that fadeth not away.

2. Catch them away before the Great Tribulation
3. Crown to be guarded
D. Christ's Promise to the Church
    1. Overcometh—make a pillar in the Temple of God, Position
    2. Overcometh—shall no more go out, Protection
    3. Overcometh—the Writings, Property
        a) The Name of God—Their Ownership
        b) The Name of the New Jerusalem—Their Citizenship
        c) The New Name of Christ—Their Future Security

"Behold, I come quickly: hold fast which thou hast, that no man take thy crown."

down out of heaven from my God: and *I will write upon him* my new name.

13 He that hath an ear, let him hear what the Spirit saith unto the churches.

14 ¶ And unto the angel of the church of the Laodiceans write; These things saith the Amen, the faithful and true witness, the beginning of the creation of God;

15 I know thy works, that thou art neither cold nor hot: I would thou wert cold or hot.

16 So then because thou art lukewarm, and neither cold nor hot, I will spue thee out of my mouth.

17 Because thou sayest, I am rich, and increased with goods, and have need of nothing; and knowest not that thou art wretched, and miserable, and poor, and blind, and naked:

18 I counsel thee to buy of me gold tried in the fire, that thou mayest be rich; and white raiment, that thou mayest be clothed, and *that* the shame of thy nakedness do not appear; and anoint thine eyes with eyesalve, that thou mayest see.

"anoint thine eyes with eyesalve, that thou mayest see."

44

The Final Church of the Seven is Laodicea—the church that receives the most scathing criticism of all. It is a picture of the final church age.

VII. Laodicea, the Apostate Church (3:14-19)
    A.   Christ's Introduction to the Church
        1. Amen—His Final Authority
        2. Faithful and True Witness—His Fair Authority
        3. Creator—the First and Foremost Authority
    B.   Christ's Complaint Against the Church
        1. Neither cold nor hot—Lukewarm
        2. Rich but poor—Lacking
        3. Unmindful of their condition—Deluded
           a) Wretched—Afflicted but not Affected
           b) Miserable—Pitiful with no Pity
           c) Poor—Physical Abundance with Spiritual Famine
           d) Blind—Seeing their Goods without seeing their Needs
           e) Naked—Clothed in Self-Righteousness instead of His Righteousness
    C.   Christ's Counsel to the Church
        1. Buy Gold Tried in the Fire—Taste His Deity
        2. Buy White Raiment—Try His Righteousness
        3. Anoint their Eyes—To Relieve the Spiritual Blindness
    D.   Christ's Caution to the Church
        1. Rebuke—Whom He Loves, He Chastens
        2. Repent—He Who Does is Forgiven

19 As many as I love, I rebuke and chasten: be zealous therefore, and repent.

20 Behold, I stand at the door, and knock: if any man hear my voice, and open the door, I will come in to him, and will sup with him, and he with me.

21 To him that overcometh will I grant to sit with me in my throne, even as I also overcame, and am set down with my Father in his throne.

22 He that hath an ear, let him hear what the Spirit saith unto the churches.

"Behold, I stand at the door, and knock"

He That Hath an Ear

THE SEVEN CHURCHES OF ASIA MINOR

1. *Ephesus, the Early Church*

2. *Smyrna, the Church in Persecution*

3. *Pergamos, the Post-Persecution Church*

4. *Thyatira, the Organized Church*

5. *Sardis, the Ritualistic Church*

6. *Philadelphia, the Revived Church*

7. *Laodicea, the Apostate Church of the End Times*

VIII. The Invitation to the Churches (3:20-22)
    A.   Christ at the Door Knocking
         1. Open for Repentance
         2. Open for Fellowship
    B.   Christ at the Door Speaking
         1. To Their Hearts—Attitude
         2. To Their Minds—Action
    C.   Christ in Heaven Promising
         1. Overcometh—Sit with Him in His Throne—Promise of Authority
         2. Overcometh—Even as He has Overcome—Promise of Accomplishment

It is evident throughout the discourse with the Seven Churches that the Heart of the Saviour is toward repentance. With almost every church, we noticed the same invitation—Repent! It is the heart's desire of Jesus Christ that we walk as closely to Him as possible. Whenever He disciplines or corrects, He makes it known that it is for our good and His love that He does so. Let us learn the lesson of repentance—a changing of the mind...of agreeing with God that His way is correct and then changing our lifestyle to match His will. While the Seven Churches were individual assemblies, they are also representative of the different stages of the Church Age:

    1) Ephesus, the Early Church
    2) Smyrna, the Church in Persecution
    3) Pergamos, the Post-Persecution Church
    4) Thyatira, the Organized Church
    5) Sardis, the Ritualistic Church
    6) Philadelphia, the Revived Church
    7) Laodicea, the Apostate Church of the End Times

While examples of each of these have existed throughout

Chapter 4

1 ¶ After this I looked, and, behold, a door *was* opened in heaven: and the first voice which I heard *was* as it were of a trumpet talking with me; which said, Come up hither, and I will shew thee things which must be hereafter.

2 And immediately I was in the spirit: and, behold, a throne was set in heaven, and *one* sat on the throne.

3 And he that sat was to look upon like a jasper and a sardine stone: and *there was* a rainbow round about the throne, in sight like unto an emerald.

4 And round about the throne *were* four and twenty seats: and upon the seats I saw four and twenty elders sitting, clothed in white raiment; and they had on their heads crowns of gold.

the ages, it is no doubt that the final stages of the Church Age are here… and we are living in them.

The fourth chapter is pronouncedly different from the previous ones. After the Church Age, we immediately have the Rapture—a catching away of the believers, as shown in the command, "Come up hither."

The Things Hereafter
Chapter 4

I.   The First Advent of the Second Coming of Christ—the Rapture (4:1-2)

    A.   The Door is Opened—God's Glory is Revealed (Compare Ezekiel 8:3)

    B.   The Voice Talking—God's Command is Given

    C.   The Trump of God—God's Communication is Clear

    D.   The Shout of the Archangel—God's Chosen Ones are Called

II.   The First Vision in Heaven—He Who Sits upon the Throne (4: 3-6)

    A.   The Perfections of His Character

        1. Jasper—The Twelfth Stone in The High Priest's Breastplate (the stone of Benjamin) Representing His Deity—White

          a) Precious

          b) Perfect

          c) Pure

        2. Sardine Stone (Sardius)—The First Stone of the High Priest's Breastplate (the stone of Reuben) Representing Judgment—Red

          a) Fiery

          b) Fearsome

          c) Final

5 And out of the throne proceeded lightnings and thunderings and voices: and *there were* seven lamps of fire burning before the throne, which are the seven Spirits of God.

6 And before the throne *there was* a sea of glass like unto crystal: and in the midst of the throne, and round about the throne, *were* four beasts full of eyes before and behind.

7 And the first beast *was* like a lion, and the second beast like a calf, and the third beast had a face as a man, and the fourth beast *was* like a flying eagle.

VISION OF THE 24 ELDERS

- *Seated on the Twenty-Four Seats*

- *Clothed in White Raiment*

- *Crowned with Crowns of Gold*

3. Rainbow
   a) Picture of the Grace of God
     (1) Realization of God's Promises
     (2) Reminder of God's Covenants
   b) Reflector of God's Mercies
   c) Emblem of the Mercy of God
     (1) Peace from God
     (2) Reconciliation to God
4. Emerald—The Fifth Stone of the High Priest's Breastplate (the stone of Judah) Representing the Goodness of God—Green
   a) Enduring—Ever Faithful
   b) Evergreen—Ever New

III. The Vision of the Twenty-four Elders (4: 4)
   A. Seated on the Twenty-four Seats
     1. Resting
     2. Reigning
     3. Rewarded
   B. Clothed in White Raiment
     1. Redeemed
     2. Righteous
     3. Rewarded
   C. Crowned with Crowns of Gold
     1. Recognized
     2. Rulers
     3. Rewarded

IV. The Vision of the Throne (4: 5-7)
   A. The Power of the Throne
     1. Lightnings
     2. Thunderings
     3. Voices
   B. The Presence of the Throne

8 ¶ And the four beasts had each of them six wings about *him*; and *they were* full of eyes within: and they rest not day and night, saying, Holy, holy, holy, Lord God Almighty, which was, and is, and is to come.

9 And when those beasts give glory and honour and thanks to him that sat on the throne, who liveth for ever and ever,

10 The four and twenty elders fall down before him that sat on the throne, and worship him that liveth for ever and ever, and cast their crowns before the throne, saying,

11 Thou art worthy, O Lord, to receive glory and honour and power: for thou hast created all things, and for thy pleasure they are and were created.

"Thou art worthy, O Lord, to receive glory and honour and power: for thou hast created all things, and for thy pleasure they are and were created."

       1. Seven Lamps—Seven Spirits of God (seven lamps of the Tabernacle were kept burning continually… see Lev. 24:2)
          a) Picture of Perfection
          b) Picture of Completion
          c) Picture of Wisdom
       2. Burning Before the Throne
          a) Continual Presence
          b) Constant Supply
          c) Complete Energy
   C. The Picture of the Throne
       1. Sea of Glass—Crystal (Clarity of Knowledge)
       2. Four Beasts—Seraphim (Isaiah 6)
          a) Before the Throne
          b) Midst of the Throne
          c) Round About the Throne

V. The Vision of the Four Beasts (4: 7-9)
   A. Their Individual Descriptions
       1. First—Face of a Lion (Kingship)
       2. Second—Face of a Calf (Humility)
       3. Third—Face of a Man (Humanity)
       4. Fourth—As a Flying Eagle (Divinity)
   B. Their Collective Descriptions
       1. Six Wings—Covering and Conveyance (see Isaiah 6)
       2. Full of Eyes—Representative of the Omniscience of God
          a) Before
          b) Behind
          c) Within
   C. Their Common Duties
       1. Ceaseless and Tireless Praise

Chapter 5

1 ¶ And I saw in the right hand of him that sat on the throne a book written within and on the backside, sealed with seven seals.

2 And I saw a strong angel proclaiming with a loud voice, Who is worthy to open the book, and to loose the seals thereof?

3 And no man in heaven, nor in earth, neither under the earth, was able to open the book, neither to look thereon.

4 And I wept much, because no man was found worthy to open and to read the book, neither to look thereon.

5 And one of the elders saith unto me, Weep not: behold, the Lion of the tribe of Juda, the Root of David, hath prevailed to open the book, and to loose the seven seals thereof.

"the Lion of the tribe of Juda, the Root of David"

2. Consecrated and Thankful Worship
3. Continual Glory and Honor to the Eternal God

VI. The Scene of Worship by the Twenty-Four Elders—Representatives of the Church (4: 10-11)
   A. Obeisance and Honor—Falling Before Him
   B. Worship—Casting Down their Crowns at His Feet
   C. Praise—Worthy to the Lamb
      1. As Creator of All Things
      2. As Cherisher of All Things

The Things Hereafter
Chapter 5

I. The Seven Sealed Book (5: 1-5)
   A. The Description of the Book
      1. Its Location—In the Right Hand of God
      2. Its Likeness—Written Within and Without (Backside)
      3. Its Lock—The Seven Seals
   B. The Dilemma of the Book
      1. Who Is Worthy to Open It?
      2. Who is Able to Loose the Seals?
   C. The Distress of the Situation
      1. No Man In Heaven to Open and Look in the Book
      2. No Man On Earth
      3. No Man Beneath the Earth
   D. The Discouragement of the Prophet—Weeping
   E. The Disclosure by the Elder
      1. "Weep Not"—Be Encouraged
      2. Worthy is One—The Lion of the Tribe of

6 ¶ And I beheld, and, lo, in the midst of the throne and of the four beasts, and in the midst of the elders, stood a Lamb as it had been slain, having seven horns and seven eyes, which are the seven Spirits of God sent forth into all the earth.

7 And he came and took the book out of the right hand of him that sat upon the throne.

8 And when he had taken the book, the four beasts and four *and* twenty elders fell down before the Lamb, having every one of them harps, and golden vials full of odours, which are the prayers of saints.

9 And they sung a new song, saying, Thou art worthy to take the book, and to open the seals thereof: for thou wast slain, and hast redeemed us to God by thy blood out of every kindred, and tongue, and people, and nation;

10 And hast made us unto our God kings and priests: and we shall reign on the earth.

11 And I beheld, and I heard the voice of many angels round about the throne and

Sing a New Song

- Praise for His Worth

- Praise for His Sacrifice

- Praise for His Redemption

- Praise for His Blood

- Praise for His Reward

56

Judah

II. The Sacrificed Saviour (5: 6-7)
   A. His Appearance
      1. Standing—Evidence of His Conclusive Victory over the Foe
      2. In the Midst—Evidence of His Constant Intimacy with the Redeemed
      3. As it had been Slain—Evidence of His Complete Suffering
      4. Seven Horns—Evidence of His Consummate Power
      5. Seven Eyes—Evidence of His Comprehensive Knowledge
   B. His Actions
      1. He Came to the Throne of God
      2. He Took the Book from the Right Hand of God

III. The Scene in Heaven Over the Taking of the Book by the Lamb (5: 8-14)
   A. Worship Participants
      1. Four Beasts
      2. Twenty-four Elders
      3. Angels
      4. Every Creature
         a) In Heaven
         b) On Earth
         c) Under the Earth
         d) In the Sea
   B. Worship Tools
      1. Harps
      2. Golden Vials Full of Odours—Prayers of the Saints
   C. Worship Practices

the beasts and the elders: and the number of them was ten thousand times ten thousand, and thousands of thousands;

12   Saying with a loud voice, Worthy is the Lamb that was slain to receive power, and riches, and wisdom, and strength, and honour, and glory, and blessing.

13   And every creature which is in heaven, and on the earth, and under the earth, and such as are in the sea, and all that are in them, heard I saying, Blessing, and honour, and glory, and power, *be* unto him that sitteth upon the throne, and unto the Lamb for ever and ever.

14   And the four beasts said, Amen. And the four *and* twenty elders fell down and worshipped him that liveth for ever and ever.

Blessing, and honour, and glory, and power

THE SEVEN WORTHIES

1. *Worthy to Receive Power*

2. *Worthy to Receive Riches*

3. *Worthy to Receive Wisdom*

4. *Worthy to Receive Strength*

5. *Worthy to Receive Honor*

6. *Worthy to Receive Glory*

7. *Worthy to Receive Blessing*

1. Fall at His Feet
2. Sing a New Song—Redeemed Only
   a) Praise for His Worth
   b) Praise for His Sacrifice
   c) Praise for Redemption
   d) Praise for His Blood
   e) Praise for His Reward
      1) He Makes us Kings
      2) He Makes us Priests
      3) He Make us Rulers
3. Shouts—by the Angels, The Seven Worthies:
   a) Worthy to Receive Power
   b) Worthy to Receive Riches
   c) Worthy to Receive Wisdom
   d) Worthy to Receive Strength
   e) Worthy to Receive Honor
   f) Worthy to Receive Glory
   g) Worthy to Receive Blessing
4. Praises—by Every Living Creature
   a) The Content of the Praise
      (1) Blessing
      (2) Honor
      (3) Glory
      (4) Power
   b) The Direction of the Praise
      (1) To the Father
      (2) To the Son
   c) The Conclusion of the Praise
      (1) Amen—So Let It Be, The Four Beasts
      (2) Worship—The Four and Twenty Elders

Chapter 6

1 ¶ And I saw when the Lamb opened one of the seals, and I heard, as it were the noise of thunder, one of the four beasts saying, Come and see.

2 And I saw, and behold a white horse: and he that sat on him had a bow; and a crown was given unto him: and he went forth conquering, and to conquer.

3 ¶ And when he had opened the second seal, I heard the second beast say, Come and see.

4 And there went out another horse *that was* red: and *power* was given to him that sat thereon to take peace from the earth, and that they should kill one another: and there was given unto him a great sword.

5 And when he had opened the third seal, I heard the third beast say, Come and see. And I beheld, and lo a black horse; and he that sat on him had a pair of balances in his hand.

6 And I heard a voice in the midst of the four beasts say, A measure of wheat for a penny, and three measures

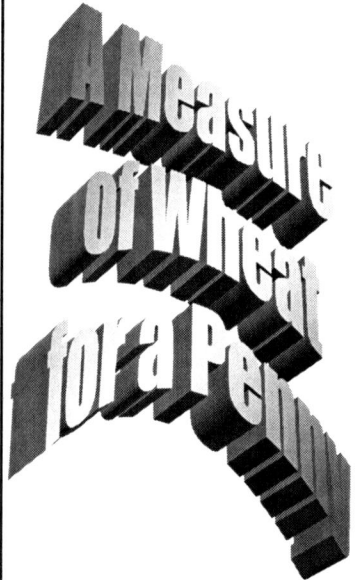

The Things Hereafter
Chapter 6
Upon the opening of each seal, John is invited to "Come and see." It is evident that we who are Raptured shall be witnesses from Heaven to the events occurring on earth.

I.   The First Seal Opened (6: 1-2)
    A.   The Description of the Open Seal
        1. White Horse—Symbol of the Anti-Christ
        2. Bow—Symbol of Power
        3. Crown—Symbol of Authority
    B.   The Distinctions of the Open Seal
        1. Going Forth—Aggressiveness
        2. To Conquer— Armed conflict

II.   The Second Seal Opened (6: 3-4)
    A.   The Description of the Open Seal
        1. Red Horse—Symbol of Chaos
        2. Great Sword—Symbol of Destruction
    B.   The Distinctions of the Open Seal
        1. Power to Take Peace—Anarchy
        2. Power to Cause Murders—Annihilation

III.   The Third Seal Opened (6: 5-6)
    A.   The Description of the Open Seal
        1. Black Horse—Desolation
        2. Pair of Balances—Symbol of Economic Judgment
    B.   The Distinctions of the Open Seal
        1. Measure of Wheat for a Penny; Three Measures of Barley for a Penny— Economic Collapse
        2. Hurt Not the Oil and Wine—Extent of Collapse, Staples only

IV.   The Fourth Seal Opened (6: 7-8)

of barley for a penny; and *see* thou hurt not the oil and the wine.

7 And when he had opened the fourth seal, I heard the voice of the fourth beast say, Come and see.

8 And I looked, and behold a pale horse: and his name that sat on him was Death, and Hell followed with him. And power was given unto them over the fourth part of the earth, to kill with sword, and with hunger, and with death, and with the beasts of the earth.

9 ¶ And when he had opened the fifth seal, I saw under the altar the souls of them that were slain for the word of God, and for the testimony which they held:

10 And they cried with a loud voice, saying, How long, O Lord, holy and true, dost thou not judge and avenge our blood on them that dwell on the earth?

11 And white robes were given unto every one of them; and it was said unto them, that they should rest yet for a little season, until their fellowservants also and their

The Seven Seals

The First Seal—The White Horse—Warfare	6:1-2
The Second Seal—Red Horse—Destruction	6:3-4
The Third Seal—Black Horse—Desolation	6:5-6
The Fourth Seal—Pale Horse—Death	6:7-8
The Fifth Seal—Martyrs Slain—Testimony	6:9-11
The Sixth Seal—Great Earthquake—Cataclysm	6:12-17
The Seventh Seal—The Seven Trumpets— Judgment	Ch. 8-9, 11 :14-15

A.   The Description of the Open Seal
    1. Pale Horse—Death
    2. Hell
B.   The Distinctions of the Open Seal
    1. ¼ of Population Slain—Extent of Power
    2. Death by:
      a) The Sword—Upheaval of Peace, Worldwide Warfare
      b) Hunger—Upheaval of Production, Worldwide Famine
      c) Death—Upheaval of Protections, Worldwide Epidemics
      d) Beasts of the Earth—Upheaval of Protocol, Worldwide Loss of Fear for Man

V.   The Fifth Seal Opened (6: 9-11)
   A.   The Description of the Seal
    1. Under the Altar—Scene Shifts to Heaven
    2. Martyrs Slain
      a) For the Word of God
      b) For their Testimony
   B.   The Distinctions of the Seal
    1. Their Concerns
      a) How Long—When is Judgment?
      b) Avenge Our Blood—Why?
      c) On Them that Dwell on Earth—On Whom
    2. Their Rewards
      a) Rest Through the Tribulation
        (1) Until Others are Martyred
        (2) Until the Time of Tribulation is Fulfilled
      b) Robed in White—Righteousness

VI.   The Sixth Seal Opened (6: 12-17)

brethren, that should be killed as they *were*, should be fulfilled.

12 And I beheld when he had opened the sixth seal, and, lo, there was a great earthquake; and the sun became black as sackcloth of hair, and the moon became as blood;

13 And the stars of heaven fell unto the earth, even as a fig tree casteth her untimely figs, when she is shaken of a mighty wind.

14 And the heaven departed as a scroll when it is rolled together; and every mountain and island were moved out of their places.

15 And the kings of the earth, and the great men, and the rich men, and the chief captains, and the mighty men, and every bondman, and every free man, hid themselves in the dens and in the rocks of the mountains;

16 And said to the mountains and rocks, Fall on us, and hide us from the face of him that sitteth on the throne, and from the wrath of the Lamb:

17 For the great day of his

Seven Types of Men

- Kings—The Rulers

- Great Men—The Famous

- Rich Men—The Wealthy

- Chief Captains—The Warriors

- Mighty Men—The Strong

- Bond Men—The Slaves

- Free Men—The Free

A. The Description of the Open Seal
    1. The Great Earthquake
        a) Sun Becomes Black as Sackcloth—Mourning
        b) Moon Becomes as Blood
    2. Stars of Heaven Fall
        a) Untimely
        b) With Ferocity
    3. Heaven Departs as a Scroll
        a) Cataclysmic Destruction
        b) Possible Nuclear Description
    4. Mountains and Islands Moved
B. The Distinctions of the Open Seal
    1. Seven Types of Men Who Hide Themselves in Dens and Rocks
        a) Kings—the Rulers
        b) Great Men—the Famous
        c) Rich Men—the Wealthy
        d) Chief Captains—the Warriors
        e) Mighty Men—the Strong
        f) Bond Men—The Slaves
        g) Free Men—The Free
    2. Desires of these Men
        a) Seeking Destruction
        b) Seeking Escape
    3. Realizations of these Men
        a) Seeing the Saviour
        b) Sensing the Judgment
        c) Seizing upon their Guilt

wrath is come; and who shall be able to stand?

Chapter 7

1 ¶ And after these things I saw four angels standing on the four corners of the earth, holding the four winds of the earth, that the wind should not blow on the earth, nor on the sea, nor on any tree.

2 And I saw another angel ascending from the east, having the seal of the living God: and he cried with a loud voice to the four angels, to whom it was given to hurt the earth and the sea,

3 Saying, Hurt not the earth, neither the sea, nor the trees, till we have sealed the servants of our God in their foreheads.

4 And I heard the number of them which were sealed: *and there were* sealed an hundred *and* forty *and* four thousand of all the tribes of the children of Israel.

5 Of the tribe of Juda *were* sealed twelve thousand. Of the tribe of Reuben *were* sealed twelve thousand. Of the tribe of Gad *were* sealed twelve thousand.

THE 144,000

1. Twelve Thousand of Judah

2. Twelve Thousand of Reuben

3. Twelve Thousand of Gad

4. Twelve Thousand of Asher

5. Twelve Thousand of Naphtali

6. Twelve Thousand of Manasseh

7. Twelve Thousand of Simeon

8. Twelve Thousand of Levi

9. Twelve Thousand of Issachar

10. Twelve Thousand of Zebulun

11. Twelve Thousand of Joseph

12. Twelve Thousand of Benjamin

The Things Hereafter—*Parenthetical*
Chapter 7

I. The Series of Fours (7: 1)
- A. The Four Angels—Instruments of God's Judgment
- B. The Four Corners of the Earth—Extent of God's Judgment
- C. The Four Winds—The Point of God's Judgment, Atmospheric Changes

II. The Fifth Angel (7: 2-8)
- A. His Origin—Arising from the East
- B. His Office—Having the Seal of God
- C. His Oration—A Loud Voice
   1. Pause the Judgment Against
      - a) The Earth
      - b) The Sea
      - c) The Trees
   2. Pause the Judgment Until the One Hundred and Forty-Four Thousand are Sealed
      - a) Twelve Thousand of Judah
      - b) Twelve Thousand of Reuben
      - c) Twelve Thousand of Gad
      - d) Twelve Thousand of Asher
      - e) Twelve Thousand of Naphtali
      - f) Twelve Thousand of Manasseh
      - g) Twelve Thousand of Simeon
      - h) Twelve Thousand of Levi
      - i) Twelve Thousand of Issachar
      - j) Twelve Thousand of Zebulun
      - k) Twelve Thousand of Joseph
      - l) Twelve Thousand of Benjamin

Two things should be noted in the listing of the Twelve

6 Of the tribe of Aser *were* sealed twelve thousand. Of the tribe of Nepthalim *were* sealed twelve thousand. Of the tribe of Manasses *were* sealed twelve thousand.

7 Of the tribe of Simeon *were* sealed twelve thousand. Of the tribe of Levi *were* sealed twelve thousand. Of the tribe of Issachar *were* sealed twelve thousand.

8 Of the tribe of Zabulon *were* sealed twelve thousand. Of the tribe of Joseph *were* sealed twelve thousand. Of the tribe of Benjamin *were* sealed twelve thousand.

9 After this I beheld, and, lo, a great multitude, which no man could number, of all nations, and kindreds, and people, and tongues, stood before the throne, and before the Lamb, clothed with white robes, and palms in their hands;

10 And cried with a loud voice, saying, Salvation to our God which sitteth upon the throne, and unto the Lamb.

11 And all the angels stood round about the throne, and *about* the elders and the four beasts, and fell before the

Two things should be noted in the listing of the Twelve Tribes. First, Judah is listed first, though Reuben is the actual first-born. (See Genesis 35:22; 49:3-4 for an explanation of why Reuben lost the rights to the status of the first-born). Second, Dan is not mentioned at all—Manasseh takes his place. (See Genesis 49:17 for the prophecy regarding Dan by his father, Jacob.)

Tribes. First, Judah is listed first, though Reuben is the actual first-born. (See Genesis 35:22; 49:3-4 for an explanation of why Reuben lost the rights to the status of the first-born). Second, Dan is not mentioned at all—Manasseh takes his place. (See Genesis 49:17 for the prophecy regarding Dan by his father, Jacob.)

III.   The Great Multitude (7: 9-10)
    A.   Their Description
        1. Accounting—Innumerable
        2. Allocation—Includes
            a) All Nations—Nationalities
            b) All Kindreds—Races
            c) All People
            d) All Tongues—Languages
        3. Adornment
            a) White Robes—Righteousness
            b) Palms in their Hands—Peace
    B.   Their Distinctions
        1. Standing before the Throne
        2. Saying with a Loud Voice
            a) Salvation to Our God—Attributing Redemption
            b) Which sitteth upon the Throne—Attributing Authority
            c) To the Lamb—Attributing Atonement to the Sacrificed Saviour

IV.   The Accompanying Scene of Worship (7:11-12)
    A.   The Participants
        1. All the Angels
        2. The Four and Twenty Elders
        3. Four Beasts
    B.   Their Performances
        1. Adoration—Fell on their Faces

throne on their faces, and worshipped God,

12 Saying, Amen: Blessing, and glory, and wisdom, and thanksgiving, and honour, and power, and might, *be* unto our God for ever and ever. Amen.

13 ¶ And one of the elders answered, saying unto me, What are these which are arrayed in white robes? and whence came they?

14 And I said unto him, Sir, thou knowest. And he said to me, These are they which came out of great tribulation, and have washed their robes, and made them white in the blood of the Lamb.

15 Therefore are they before the throne of God, and serve him day and night in his temple: and he that sitteth on the throne shall dwell among them.

16 They shall hunger no more, neither thirst any more; neither shall the sun light on them, nor any heat.

17 For the Lamb which is in the midst of the throne shall feed them, and shall lead them unto living fountains of waters: and God shall wipe

THE SEVEN ACCLAMATIONS

1. Blessing

2. Glory

3. Wisdom

4. Thanksgiving

5. Honor

6. Power

7. Might

2. Agreement—"Amen"
3. Seven Acclamations
   a) Blessing
   b) Glory
   c) Wisdom
   d) Thanksgiving
   e) Honor
   f) Power
   g) Might

V. The Explanation by the Elder (7: 13-17)
   A. The Questions to John
      1. Who Are These in White Robes?
      2. Where Did They Come From?
   B. The Response from John
      1. Assertion of Ignorance on his Part
      2. Assurance of Knowledge on the Elder's Part
   C. The Answer from the Elder
      1. They who Came Out of the Great Tribulation—Results of Martyrdom
      2. They who Washed their Robes White in the Blood of the Lamb—Redeemed by the Lamb
      3. They who are Before the Throne— Relationship with the Father
      4. They who Serve God Night and Day— Responsibility to the Father
      5. They who Shall No Longer Suffer— Reward from the Father
         a) No Hunger—the Bread of Life
         b) No Thirst—the Water of Life
         c) No Night or Light—the Light of the World

away all tears from their
eyes.

Chapter 8

1 ¶ And when he had opened
the seventh seal, there was
silence in heaven about the
space of half an hour.
2 And I saw the seven angels
which stood before God; and
to them were given seven
trumpets.
3 And another angel came and
stood at the altar, having a
golden censer; and there was
given unto him much in-
cense, that he should offer *it*
with the prayers of all saints
upon the golden altar which
was before the throne.
4 And the smoke of the incense,
which came with the prayers
of the saints, ascended up before God out of the angel's
hand.
5 And the angel took the censer,
and filled it with fire of the
altar, and cast *it* into the
earth: and there were voices,
and thunderings, and lightnings, and an earthquake.

"There was silence in heaven about the space of half an hour"

d) No Heat
6. They who Shall Receive Promises
   a) He Shall Dwell Among Them— Presence
   b) He Shall Feed Them—Provision
   c) He Shall Lead Them—Protection, Living Fountains
   d) He Shall Comfort Them—Pleasure, Wipe Away Tears

The Things Hereafter
Chapter 8

I.   The Seventh Seal Opened (8: 1-5)

A.   The Silence—about a Half Hour

B.   The Scene
1. Seven Angels
2. Seven Trumpets

C.   The Servant—the Eighth Angel
1. His Description
   a) Standing at the Altar
   b) Censer in Hand
   c) Substantial Incense
2. His Duties
   a) Offer Incense
      (1) With the Prayers of the Saints
      (2) Upon the Golden Altar Before the Throne
   b) Fill the Censer
      (1) With Fire From the Altar
      (2) Cast it Down to Earth
         (a) Voices
         (b) Thunderings
         (c) Lightnings

6 And the seven angels which had the seven trumpets prepared themselves to sound.

7 ¶ The first angel sounded, and there followed hail and fire mingled with blood, and they were cast upon the earth: and the third part of trees was burnt up, and all green grass was burnt up.

8 And the second angel sounded, and as it were a great mountain burning with fire was cast into the sea: and the third part of the sea became blood;

9 And the third part of the creatures which were in the sea, and had life, died; and the third part of the ships were destroyed.

10 And the third angel sounded, and there fell a great star from heaven, burning as it were a lamp, and it fell upon the third part of the rivers, and upon the fountains of waters;

11 And the name of the star is called Wormwood: and the third part of the waters became wormwood; and many men died of the waters, because they were made bitter.

12 And the fourth angel

The Seven Trumpets

The First Trumpet—Hail & Fire Mingled w/blood—1/3 of green grass & trees destroyed	8:7
The Second Trumpet— Great Mountain burning w/fire—1/3 of sea becomes blood; 1/3 of marine life and 1/3 of all ships destroyed	8:8-9
The Third Trumpet—The Great Star, Wormwood— Fresh waters and springs polluted, many die	8:10-11
The Fourth Trumpet— Sun, Moon, Stars—1/3 of heavenly bodies darkened	8:12
The Fifth Trumpet—(The First Woe) The Fallen Star, Abaddon/Apollyon—loosing the minions of Hell (the terrible locusts)	9:1-12
The Sixth Trumpet—(The Second Woe) The Four Angels bound in the Euphrates are loosed— sent to kill 1/3 of earth's population	9:13-21
The Seventh Trumpet— (The Third Woe) The Adoration of the Savior and the Anger of the Nations	11:14-19

(d) Earthquake
II. Seven Angels Sound the Seven Trumpets
   A. The First Angel's Trumpet (8: 7)
      1. The First Angel's Object of Judgment
         a) Hail and Fire
         b) Mingled with Blood
      2. The First Angel's Objectives of Judgment
         a) Third Part of Trees
         b) All Green Grass
   B. The Second Angel's Trumpet (8: 8-9)
      1. The Second Angel's Object of Judgment
         a) Great Mountain
         b) Burning with Fire
      2. The Second Angel's Objectives of Judgment
         a) Third Part of the Sea Became Blood
         b) Third Part of Marine Life Perish
         c) Third Part of All Ships Destroyed
   C. The Third Angel's Trumpet (8: 10-11)
      1. The Third Angel's Object of Judgment
         a) Great Star Wormwood (Bitterness)
         b) Burning as a Lamp
      2. The Third Angel's Objectives of Judgment
         a) Fresh Water Rivers
         b) Fresh Water Springs
         c) Many Men Die
   D. The Fourth Angel's Trumpet (8:12)
      1. The Fourth Angel's Objects of Judgment
         a) Sun
         b) Moon
         c) Stars
2. The Fourth Angel's Objectives of Judg-

sounded, and the third part of the sun was smitten, and the third part of the moon, and the third part of the stars; so as the third part of them was darkened, and the day shone not for a third part of it, and the night likewise.

13 And I beheld, and heard an angel flying through the midst of heaven, saying with a loud voice, Woe, woe, woe, to the inhabiters of the earth by reason of the other voices of the trumpet of the three angels, which are yet to sound!

Chapter 9

1 ¶ And the fifth angel sounded, and I saw a star fall from heaven unto the earth: and to him was given the key of the bottomless pit.

2 And he opened the bottomless pit; and there arose a smoke out of the pit, as the smoke of a great furnace; and the sun and the air were darkened by reason of the smoke of the pit.

3 And there came out of the smoke locusts upon the

ment
- a) Third Part of Heavenly Bodies Darkened
- b) Third Part of Day Darkened
- c) Third Part of Night Eliminated

E. The Three Woes (8: 13)
1. The Messenger—the Flying Angel
2. The Method—the Loud Voice
3. The Message—Woe, Woe, Woe, signifying the Severity of Judgment

The Things Hereafter
Chapter 9

I. The Fifth Angel's Trumpet (9: 1-12)—The First Woe
A. The Fallen Star—Satan Himself, (Abaddon, Apollyon—the Destroyer)
1. His Authority—Key to the Bottomless Pit
2. His Aim—To Loose the Powers of Hell (see II Peter 2:4; Jude 1:6)
3. His Attack—Against those who Have Not the Seal of God in their Foreheads
B. The Fierce Creatures—the Locusts
1. Their Description
- a) Their Shape—As Horses Prepared for Battle, Their Frightful Force
- b) Their Heads—As Crowns of Gold, Their False Claims to Deity
- c) Their Faces—As the Faces of Men, Their Facade of Friendship
- d) Their Hair—As the Hair of Women, Their Fashion of Rebellion
- e) Their Teeth—As the Teeth of Lions, Their Ferocity

earth: and unto them was given power, as the scorpions of the earth have power.

4 And it was commanded them that they should not hurt the grass of the earth, neither any green thing, neither any tree; but only those men which have not the seal of God in their foreheads.

5 And to them it was given that they should not kill them, but that they should be tormented five months: and their torment *was* as the torment of a scorpion, when he striketh a man.

6 And in those days shall men seek death, and shall not find it; and shall desire to die, and death shall flee from them.

7 And the shapes of the locusts *were* like unto horses prepared unto battle; and on their heads *were* as it were crowns like gold, and their faces *were* as the faces of men.

8 And they had hair as the hair of women, and their teeth were as *the teeth* of lions.

9 And they had breastplates, as it were breastplates of iron; and the sound of their wings *was* as the sound of chariots

"The pattern for the Three Woes coincides with the Fifth, Sixth, and Seventh Trumpets. Their special attention is God's way of stressing the dreadful events of the final three trumpets."

78

    f) Their Covering—As Breastplates of Iron, Their Formidable Preparation

    g) Their Wings—As the Sound of Chariots and Horses Going to Battle, Their Fear Upon Mankind

    h) Their Tails—As the Tails of Scorpions, Their Formula for Inflicting Pain

  C. Their Fearsome Command

   1. Their Limitations

    a) Hurt Not the Grass or the Green Things

    b) Hurt Not the Trees

    c) Hurt Not the Elect

   2. Their License

    a) Torment but Do Not Kill Torture for Five Months

    b) The Fleeing of Death—Sought, but not Found

The pattern for the Three Woes coincides with the Fifth, Sixth, and Seventh Trumpets. Their special attention is God's way of stressing the dreadful events of the final three trumpets. While there is no way that we can possibly understand the continuing horrors of the Great Tribulation, it is quite evident that the longer the Tribulation lasts, the more horrible it will become. No wonder the Scriptures record, "but for the elect's sake those days shall be shortened." (Matthew 24:22)

II. The Sixth Angel's Trumpet (9:13-21)—The Second Woe

  A. The Four Angels

   1. Their Origin—Bound in the Euphrates

2. Their Opening—Loosed by the Sixth

of many horses running to battle.

10 And they had tails like unto scorpions, and there were stings in their tails: and their power *was* to hurt men five months.

11 And they had a king over them, *which is* the angel of the bottomless pit, whose name in the Hebrew tongue *is* Abaddon, but in the Greek tongue hath *his* name Apollyon.

12 One woe is past; *and*, behold, there come two woes more hereafter.

13 ¶ And the sixth angel sounded, and I heard a voice from the four horns of the golden altar which is before God,

14 Saying to the sixth angel which had the trumpet, Loose the four angels which are bound in the great river Euphrates.

15 And the four angels were loosed, which were prepared for an hour, and a day, and a month, and a year, for to slay the third part of men.

16 And the number of the army of the horsemen *were* two hundred thousand thousand: and I heard the number of them

17 And thus I saw the horses in the vision, and them that sat on them, having breastplates of fire, and of jacinth, and brimstone: and the heads of the horses *were* as the heads of lions; and out of their mouths issued fire and smoke and brimstone.

18 By these three was the third part of men killed, by the fire, and by the smoke, and by the brimstone, which issued out of their mouths.

19 For their power is in their mouth, and in their tails: for their tails *were* like unto serpents, and had heads, and with them they do hurt.

20 And the rest of the men which were not killed by these plagues yet repented not of the works of their hands, that they should not worship devils, and idols of gold, and silver, and brass, and stone, and of wood: which neither can see, nor hear, nor walk:

Angel

   3. Their Office

      a) Prepared for One Year, One Month, One Day and One Hour

      b) Sent to Kill One Third of Mankind

B.   The Two Hundred Million Man Army

   1. Arising from the East—Probably Chinese

   2. Allying Against the Anti-Christ

C.   The Deadly Horses

   1. Their Features

      a) Breastplates of

         (1) Fire

         (2) Jacinth—Black Red

         (3) Brimstone

      b) Heads as Heads of Lions

      c) Mouths Issuing

         (1) Fire

         (2) Smoke

         (3) Brimstone

   2. Their Function

      a) To Hurt Men with

         (1) Their Heads

         (2) Their Mouths

         (3) Their Tails

      b) To Kill a Third Part of Mankind (in conjunction with the Four Angels and the Great Army of 200,000,000)

D.   The Response of the Survivors

   1. No Turning to God in Repentance for Sins

   2. No Turning from Sins Being Practiced

      a) Spiritual—Idolatry

      b) Physical

         (1) Murders, literally Slaughterings

21 Neither repented they of their murders, nor of their sorceries, nor of their fornication, nor of their thefts.

Chapter 10

1 ¶ And I saw another mighty angel come down from heaven, clothed with a cloud: and a rainbow *was* upon his head, and his face *was* as it were the sun, and his feet as pillars of fire:

2 And he had in his hand a little book open: and he set his right foot upon the sea, and *his* left *foot* on the earth,

3 And cried with a loud voice, as *when* a lion roareth: and when he had cried, seven thunders uttered their voices.

4 And when the seven thunders had uttered their voices, I was about to write: and I heard a voice from heaven saying unto me, Seal up those things which the seven thunders uttered, and write them not.

5 And the angel which I saw stand upon the sea and upon the earth lifted up his hand to heaven,

6 And sware by him that liveth

"he had in his hand a little book"

(2) Sorceries—Greek φαρμακειων
"pharmacy" literally the use or ad-
ministering of drugs

(3) Fornication—Greek πορνεια
"pornography"—sexual sins

(4) Thefts

The Things Hereafter--*Parenthetical*
Chapter 10

I. The Mighty Angel—Jesus Christ, His Seven Attributes (10: 1-3)

    A.   Come Down from Heaven—His Arrival

    B.   Clothed with a Cloud—His Acclaim

    C.   Crowned with a Rainbow—His Assurance

    D.   Countenance as the Sun—His Ardor

    E.   Conveyance (Feet) as Pillars of Fire—His Ad-
monition

    F.   Carrying the Little Book—His Authority

    G.   Crying with a Loud Voice as a Lion—His
Awesome Majesty

II. The Little Book (10: 2)

    A.   Held in the Mighty Angel's Hand—All Secu-
rity Retained

    B.   Held Open—All Secrets Revealed

III. The Seven Thunders (10: 3-4)

    A.   Sounded upon the Voice of the Mighty Angel

    B.   Sealed by a Voice From Heaven

IV. The Mighty Angel—His Actions (10:5-7)

    A.   Stands Upon the Sea and the Earth—
Comprehensive Authority

    B.   Lifts His Hand to Heaven—Confident Agree-
ment

    C.   Swears to the God of Heaven—Complete Alfor ever and ever, who created heaven, and the things that therein are, and the earth, and the things that therein are, and the sea, and the things which are therein, that there should be time no longer:

7 But in the days of the voice of the seventh angel, when he shall begin to sound, the mystery of God should be finished, as he hath declared to his servants the prophets.

8 ¶ And the voice which I heard from heaven spake unto me again, and said, Go *and* take the little book which is open in the hand of the angel which standeth upon the sea and upon the earth.

9 And I went unto the angel, and said unto him, Give me the little book. And he said unto me, Take *it,* and eat it up; and it shall make thy belly bitter, but it shall be in thy mouth sweet as honey.

10 And I took the little book out of the angel's hand, and ate it up; and it was in my mouth sweet as honey: and as soon as I had eaten it, my belly was bitter.

11 And he said unto me, Thou

8 But thou, son of man, hear what I say unto thee; Be not thou rebellious like that rebellious house: open thy mouth, and eat that I give thee.

9 And when I looked, behold, an hand *was* sent unto me; and, lo, a roll of a book *was* therein;

10 And he spread it before me; and it *was* written within and without: and *there was* written therein lamentations, and mourning, and woe.

1 ¶ Moreover he said unto me, Son of man, eat that thou findest; eat this roll, and go speak unto the house of Israel.

2 So I opened my mouth, and he caused me to eat that roll.

3 And he said unto me, Son of man, cause thy belly to eat, and fill thy bowels with this roll that I give thee. Then did I eat *it*; and it was in my mouth as honey for sweetness.

4 And he said unto me, Son of man, go, get thee unto the house of Israel, and speak with my words unto them.

legiance (see Hebrews 6:13 for an explanation for why this is Jesus Christ)
1. The Eternal One
2. The Establishing One—Creator
D. Announces the Coming End of Time— Consummate Aftermath
1. Its Precedent—the Third Woe
2. Its Presentation—the Mystery of God Finished
3. Its Timing—After the Fulfillment of Prophecy
V. The Fate of the Little Book (10: 8-11)
A. John is Commanded to Take the Book
1. Distinguished as the Open Book—As to Prophecy Foretold
2. Designated as the Book in the Mighty Angel's Hand—As to Promises Fulfilled
3. Described with the Angel which Stood Upon the Sea and Earth—As to Power Featured
B. John is Commanded to Eat the Book (compare Ezekiel 2:8-3:4)
1. Sweet to the Lips—Sweet Word of God
2. Bitter to the Belly—The Bitter Judgment in the Word of God
C. John is Commanded to Prophesy
1. After the Consuming of the Word of God—the Power of Preaching
2. Again as Before—the Perseverance of Preaching
3. At the People, Nations, Tongues, and Kings of the Earth—the Point of Preaching
While Chapters 10 and 11 are both parenthetical chapters

must prophesy again before many peoples, and nations, and tongues, and kings.

Chapter 11

1 ¶ And there was given me a reed like unto a rod: and the angel stood, saying, Rise, and measure the temple of God, and the altar, and them that worship therein.

2 But the court which is without the temple leave out, and measure it not; for it is given unto the Gentiles: and the holy city shall they tread under foot forty *and* two months.

3 ¶ And I will give *power* unto my two witnesses, and they shall prophesy a thousand two hundred *and* threescore days, clothed in sackcloth.

4 These are the two olive trees, and the two candlesticks standing before the God of the earth.

5 And if any man will hurt them, fire proceedeth out of their mouth, and devoureth their enemies: and if any man will hurt them, he must in this manner be killed.

6 These have power to shut

THE TWO WITNESSES

- *Referred to as the two olive trees—their Anointing*

- *Referred to as the two candlesticks—their Assignment*

- *Representative of the Law and the Prophets*

- *Their identity—Moses, as a representative of the Witness of the Law; Elijah, as a representative of the Witness of the Prophets*

- *Raptured as a Witness that culminates in the conversion of the 144,000 end time witnesses*

(Chapter 11 up through verse 13), they deal with two very different subjects and time periods. Chapter 10 takes us up to the near end of the Tribulation, while Chapter 11: 1-13 takes us back through the first three and a half years right up to the mid-point of the Great Tribulation. Chapter 10 introduces us to the Mighty Angel—Jesus Christ Himself (focusing mostly on a Heavenly Scene); Chapter 11 introduces us to the Two Mighty Witnesses (focusing mainly on earthly events). Chapter 11 will continue with the Seventh Angel in the Third Woe. Things on earth will grow worse and worse.

The Things Hereafter
Chapter 11

I.   The Command to Measure (11: 1-2)
   A.   Measure
      1. The Temple—Rebuilt as Promised
      2. The Altar—Restoration of Sacrifices
      3. The Worshippers—Return to Orthodoxy
   B.   Measure Not—The Outer Court
      1. Given over to the Gentiles
      2. Overrun for 3 ½ Years

II.   The Two Witnesses (11: 3-12)
   A.   Their Life
      1. Their Period—(3 ½ Years)—Practicing Faithfulness
      2. Their Presence—Clothed in Sackcloth, Preaching Repentance
      3. Their Prophecy—See Zechariah 4, Prophecy Fulfilled
         a) Two Olive Trees, Depicting Their Anointing—a Testimony from God
         b) Two Candlesticks, Depicting Their Assignment—a Testimony before Men

heaven, that it rain not in the days of their prophecy: and have power over waters to turn them to blood, and to smite the earth with all plagues, as often as they will.

7 And when they shall have finished their testimony, the beast that ascendeth out of the bottomless pit shall make war against them, and shall overcome them, and kill them.

8 And their dead bodies *shall lie* in the street of the great city, which spiritually is called Sodom and Egypt, where also our Lord was crucified.

9 And they of the people and kindreds and tongues and nations shall see their dead bodies three days and an half, and shall not suffer their dead bodies to be put in graves.

10 And they that dwell upon the earth shall rejoice over them, and make merry, and shall send gifts one to another; because these two prophets tormented them that dwelt on the earth.

11 And after three days and an half the Spirit of life from God entered into them, and

"And their dead bodies *shall lie* in the street of the great city, which spiritually is called Sodom and Egypt, where also our Lord was crucified."

      4. Their Powers, Proving Authority
         a) Breathing Fire—Protection against Foes
         b) Mirroring Hurt—Punishing Persecutors
         c) Turning Water into Blood— Impairing the Sinners
         d) Smiting Plagues At Will—Providing Punishments

B.   Their Death
    1. Their Ancient Enemy—The Beast, Satan Himself
       a) His Ascension—the Bottomless Pit
       b) His Animosity—Hatred for the Faithful Witnesses
       c) His Anger—Murder of the Witnesses
    2. Their Apparent End
       a) Their Finish—Lying Dead
          (1) In the Streets of Jerusalem
             (a) Spiritually called Sodom— Covenant Breakers
             (b) Spiritually called Egypt— Rejecters of His Testimonies
          (2) For 3 ½ Days
       b) Their Fate
          (1) Seen of the World
          (2) Suffered Not to be Buried
          (3) Celebrations upon Their Death
       c) Their Future
          (1) Resurrected before Men
          (2) Ascended up to Heaven
          (3) Beheld by their Enemies

III.   The Great Earthquake (11: 13)

they stood upon their feet; and great fear fell upon them which saw them.

12 And they heard a great voice from heaven saying unto them, Come up hither. And they ascended up to heaven in a cloud; and their enemies beheld them.

13 And the same hour was there a great earthquake, and the tenth part of the city fell, and in the earthquake were slain of men seven thousand: and the remnant were affrighted, and gave glory to the God of heaven.

14 ¶ The second woe is past; *and*, behold, the third woe cometh quickly.

15 And the seventh angel sounded; and there were great voices in heaven, saying, The kingdoms of this world are become *the kingdoms* of our Lord, and of his Christ; and he shall reign for ever and ever.

16 And the four and twenty elders, which sat before God on their seats, fell upon their faces, and worshipped God,

17 Saying, We give thee thanks, O Lord God Almighty, which art, and wast, and art

**The Third Woe
(The Seventh Trumpet)**

A. Its Timing—The Ascension of the Two Witnesses
B. Its Effects
   1. Tenth Part of City Falls
   2. Seven Thousand Men Slain
   3. Remnant Frightened
   4. Remnant Gives Glory to God

IV. The Seventh Angel's Trumpet—(11: 14-19) The Third Woe
   A. The Announcement of the Great Voices
      1. Kingdoms of this World are become the Kingdoms of our Lord, and of His Christ—The Supremacy of His Might
      2. He Shall Reign Forever and Ever—The Scope of His Majesty
   B. The Adoration of the Twenty-Four Elders
      1. Worship to God
      2. Thanks to God
         a) For His Personality
         b) For His Power
         c) For His Prestige
   C. The Anger of the Nations
      1. At His Punishment
      2. At His Judgment
         a) To the Wicked, Retribution
         b) To the Righteous, Reward
            (1) Prophets
            (2) Saints
            (3) All Who Reverence God
   D. The Attention to the Temple
      1. Ark of the Testament—The Pattern of His Salvation—The Gospel
      2. Lightnings—The Piercing Effect of the

to come; because thou hast taken to thee thy great power, and hast reigned.

18 And the nations were angry, and thy wrath is come, and the time of the dead, that they should be judged, and that thou shouldest give reward unto thy servants the prophets, and to the saints, and them that fear thy name, small and great; and shouldest destroy them which destroy the earth.

19 And the temple of God was opened in heaven, and there was seen in his temple the ark of his testament: and there were lightnings, and voices, and thunderings, and an earthquake, and great hail.

Chapter 12

1 ¶ And there appeared a great wonder in heaven; a woman clothed with the sun, and the moon under her feet, and upon her head a crown of twelve stars:

2 And she being with child cried, travailing in birth, and pained to be delivered.

3 And there appeared another

The Great Red Dragon

Gospel

3. Voices—The Proclamation of the Gospel
4. Thunderings—The Power of the Gospel
5. Earthquake—The Potent Changing Ability of the Gospel
6. Great Hail—The Punishing Effect For The Rejection Of The Gospel

The Things Hereafter
Chapter 12

I.   The First Wonder in Heaven—the Woman (12:1-2)

    A.   Her Appearance

        1. Clothed With the Sun
        2. Moon Under Her Feet
        3. Crowned With Twelve Stars

    B.   Her Anguish—with Child

        1. In Tears
        2. In Travail
        3. In Turmoil

II.   The Second Wonder in Heaven—The Great Red Dragon (12: 3-4)

    A.   His Appearance

        1. Seven Heads—Dominions
        2. Ten Horns—Dominance
        3. Seven Crowns—Diadems

    B.   His Actions

        1. Casts the Third Part of Stars to Earth—Angels that are Fallen
        2. Stands before the Woman—Adversary, Ever Vigilant and Ready to Destroy
        3. To Devour the Child as soon as it is Born—Anti-Christ, the Spirit that Seeks to Destroy the Christ

wonder in heaven; and behold a great red dragon, having seven heads and ten horns, and seven crowns upon his heads.

4 And his tail drew the third part of the stars of heaven, and did cast them to the earth: and the dragon stood before the woman which was ready to be delivered, for to devour her child as soon as it was born.

5 And she brought forth a man child, who was to rule all nations with a rod of iron: and her child was caught up unto God, and *to* his throne.

6 And the woman fled into the wilderness, where she hath a place prepared of God, that they should feed her there a thousand two hundred *and* threescore days.

7 And there was war in heaven: Michael and his angels fought against the dragon; and the dragon fought and his angels,

8 And prevailed not; neither was their place found any more in heaven.

9 And the great dragon was cast out, that old serpent, called the Devil, and Satan, which

THE SEVEN

CONSEQUENCES

OF THE WAR

IN HEAVEN

- *Praise in Heaven*
- *Power of the Overcomers*
- *Presence of the Dragon*
- *Persecution of the Woman*
- *Pursuit of the Serpent*
- *Protection of the Earth*
- *Persecution of the Remnant*

III. The War of the Wonders (12: 5-17)
   A.   The Birth of the Man Child—Jesus Christ, a Historical Event
   B.   The Ascension of the Son—Caught Up to God—A Documented Occurrence
   C.   The Fleeing Woman—the Nation of Israel—A Coming Event
      1. To a Place Prepared—the Promise of Protection
      2. For a Time Prescribed—the Promise of Protraction, 3 ½ Years (see Matthew 24: 22)
   D.   The War in Heaven
      1. The Combatants of the Battle
         a) Michael the Archangel
         b) Heavenly Angelic Army
         c) The Dragon—Satan
         d) The Demonic Army of Satan
      2. The Conduct of the Battle
         a) Satan's Power Does Not Prevail—the Promise of Success
         b) Satan's Place is Lost—The Promise of Separation
         c) Satan's Person and His Army are Cast Out—the Promise of Subjugation
      3. The Seven Consequences of the Battle
         a) The Praise in Heaven for
            (1) Salvation
            (2) Strength
            (3) Kingdom of God
            (4) Power of Christ
            (5) Defeat of the Accuser
         b) The Power of the Overcomers

deceiveth the whole world: he was cast out into the earth, and his angels were cast out with him.

10 And I heard a loud voice saying in heaven, Now is come salvation, and strength, and the kingdom of our God, and the power of his Christ: for the accuser of our brethren is cast down, which accused them before our God day and night.

11 And they overcame him by the blood of the Lamb, and by the word of their testimony; and they loved not their lives unto the death.

12 ¶ Therefore rejoice, *ye* heavens, and ye that dwell in them. Woe to the inhabiters of the earth and of the sea! for the devil is come down unto you, having great wrath, because he knoweth that he hath but a short time.

13 And when the dragon saw that he was cast unto the earth, he persecuted the woman which brought forth the man *child*.

14 And to the woman were given two wings of a great eagle, that she might fly into the wilderness, into her

"And they overcame him by the blood of the Lamb, and by the word of their testimony; and they loved not their lives unto the death"

      (1) The Blood of the Lamb—Their Application
      (2) Word of their Testimony—Their Achievement
      (3) Selfless Love—Their Attitude
  c) The Presence of the Dragon
      (1) From Heaven to Earth—His Downfall
      (2) From Accusation to Persecution—His Destructive Character
  d) The Persecution of the Woman
      (1) Given Power to Fly (Two Great Wings)—Speaks to the Swiftness of Her Protection
      (2) Given Her Place—Speaks to the Preparation of Her Protection
      (3) Given Her Provision—Speaks to the Process of Her Protection
  e) The Pursuit of the Serpent (the Great Dragon)—the Great Flood
  f) The Protection of the Earth—Opens to Swallow the Flood Waters
  g) The Persecution of the Remnant
      (1) Wrath against the Keepers of the Commandments—144,000
      (2) War against those with the Testimony of Jesus Christ—Converts of the 144,000

Chapter 12 dealt with both historical facts (birth and ascension of Jesus Christ) and prophetical fact. There is actually no difference between the two. We are confined to time as human beings, but God is not so confined. When

place, where she is nour-
ished for a time, and times,
and half a time, from the face
of the serpent.

15 And the serpent cast out of
his mouth water as a flood
after the woman, that he
might cause her to be carried
away of the flood.

16 And the earth helped the
woman, and the earth
opened her mouth, and swallowed up the flood which
the dragon cast out of his
mouth.

17 And the dragon was wroth
with the woman, and went
to make war with the rem-
nant of her seed, which keep
the commandments of God,
and have the testimony of Jesus Christ.

Chapter 13

1 ¶ And I stood upon the sand
of the sea, and saw a beast
rise up out of the sea, having
seven heads and ten horns,
and upon his horns ten
crowns, and upon his heads
the name of blasphemy.

2 And the beast which I saw
was like unto a leopard, and
his feet were as *the feet* of a

δυναμις

εξουσιαν

Power

and

Authority

He looks at such events, He does not see them as past facts and future possibilities. Future events are just as much reliable facts with God as documented history is to us. We should take care not to fall into the fallacy that these are events that might be—they are fore-stated facts before they occur. They are evidences of pre-recorded history.

The Things Hereafter
Chapter 13

I.   The Beast Rising Out of the Sea (13: 1-10)
- A.   His Description (Compare Rev. 17)
  1. Seven Heads with the Name of Blasphemy
  2. Ten Horns with Ten Crowns
- B.   His Disposition
  1. Overall—Leopard-like, As to His Persuasive Ferocity
  2. Feet—Bear-like, As to His Powerful Defenses
  3. Mouth—Lion-like, As to His Potent Strength
- C.   His Decree
  1. His Power—δυναμις, power
  2. His Position, seat
  3. His Prestige—εξουσιαν, great authority
- D.   His Deadly Wound
  1. The Head Wounded Unto Death
  2. The Healing of the Deadly Wound
  3. The Homage to the Beast & to the Dragon
     a) Worshipping His Person
     b) Worshipping His Power
- E.   His Duties

bear, and his mouth as the mouth of a lion: and the dragon gave him his power, and his seat, and great authority.

3 And I saw one of his heads as it were wounded to death; and his deadly wound was healed: and all the world wondered after the beast.

4 And they worshipped the dragon which gave power unto the beast: and they worshipped the beast, saying, Who *is* like unto the beast? who is able to make war with him?

5 And there was given unto him a mouth speaking great things and blasphemies; and power was given unto him to continue forty *and* two months.

6 And he opened his mouth in blasphemy against God, to blaspheme his name, and his tabernacle, and them that dwell in heaven.

7 And it was given unto him to make war with the saints, and to overcome them: and power was given him over all kindreds, and tongues, and nations.

8 And all that dwell upon the

"And they worshipped the dragon which gave power unto the beast: and they worshipped the beast, saying, Who *is* like unto the beast? who is able to make war with him?"

1. Ability to Speak Great Lies and Promises
2. Ability to Speak Great Blasphemies
3. Anarchy Against God's Authority
   a) Against His Name—His Attributes
   b) Against His Tabernacle—His Abode
   c) Against His Saints—His Atoned
4. Authority to Sustain for 3 ½ Years

F. His Destructive Nature
1. Makes War with the Saints
2. Power Over the World
   a) All Kindreds
   b) All Tongues
   c) All Nations

G. His Due
1. Worship from the Then Present Lost World—Those Whose Names are not Written in the Lamb's Book of Life
2. Warning to the Present Population—He that Hath an Ear, Let Him Hear
3. Wariness of the Saints—Patience and Faith to Not Worship the Beast

II. The Beast Rising Out of the Earth (13: 11-18)

BLASPHEMY AGAINST GOD

earth shall worship him, whose names are not written in the book of life of the Lamb slain from the foundation of the world.

9 If any man have an ear, let him hear.

10 He that leadeth into captivity shall go into captivity: he that killeth with the sword must be killed with the sword. Here is the patience and the faith of the saints.

11 ¶ And I beheld another beast coming up out of the earth; and he had two horns like a lamb, and he spake as a dragon.

12 And he exerciseth all the power of the first beast before him, and causeth the earth and them which dwell therein to worship the first beast, whose deadly wound was healed.

13 And he doeth great wonders, so that he maketh fire come down from heaven on the earth in the sight of men,

14 And deceiveth them that dwell on the earth by *the means of* those miracles which he had power to do in the sight of the beast; saying to them that dwell on the

"he maketh fire come down from heaven on the earth in the sight of men"

A.　His Appearance
　　1. Two Horns Like a Lamb
　　2. Voice Like a Dragon
B.　His Authority
　　1. Of the First Beast
　　　a) In Power
　　　b) In Precedence
　　2. Of the Forced Worship
　　　a) Its Participants—All that dwell in his kingdom
　　　b) Its Point—the Beast whose deadly wound was healed
　　3. Of the Fascinating Wonders
　　　a) Fire Coming Down from Heaven—his imitation of the Authority of God
　　　b) Forceful Miracles—his imitation of the Power of God
　　　c) Fashioning of the Image—his imitation of the Worship of God
　　　d) False Resurrection—his imitation of the Victory of God
　　　e) Fallacious Life-Giving Ability to speak—his imitation of the Living Word of God
　　　f) Fierce Coercion to Worship—his imitation of the Grace of God
　　　g) Forced Marks of Identification—his imitation of the　Seal of God's Holy Spirit
　　　　(1) All must receive it
　　　　　(a) Rich or Poor
　　　　　(b) Bond or Free
　　　　(2) It must be prominently displayed

earth, that they should make an image to the beast, which had the wound by a sword, and did live.

15 And he had power to give life unto the image of the beast, that the image of the beast should both speak, and cause that as many as would not worship the image of the beast should be killed.

16 And he causeth all, both small and great, rich and poor, free and bond, to receive a mark in their right hand, or in their foreheads:

17 And that no man might buy or sell, save he that had the mark, or the name of the beast, or the number of his name.

18 Here is wisdom. Let him that hath understanding count the number of the beast: for it is the number of a man; and his number *is* Six hundred threescore *and* six.

Chapter 14

1 ¶And I looked, and, lo, a Lamb stood on the mount Sion, and with him an hundred forty *and* four thousand, having his Father's

144,000

Witnesses

    (a) In the right hand, or
    (b) In the forehead
   (3) It will be required to
    (a) Buy—as a Consumer
    (b) Sell—as Tradesman
   (4) It must be:
    (a) The Mark of the Beast
    (b) The Name of the Beast
    (c) The Number of His Name—666

*Though speculation has surrounded these three Greek letters for hundreds of years (chi xi stigma—the 22nd, 14th and an obsolete letter of the Greek alphabet), we can be sure of this one thing—this number **will** be the mark of the beast. All who receive it will be under the judgment of God—with no hope of salvation.*

The Things Hereafter
Chapter 14

I. The Powerful Victory of the Lamb (14:1)
  A. His Position, Standing—Evidence of the Fulfillment of Power
  B. His Presence, On Mount Zion—Evidence of the Fulfillment of Promise
  C. His Procession, With the 144,000—Evidence of the Fulfillment of Protection
  D. His Pattern—With the Father's Seal
II. The Possession of the Lamb—the 144,000 Protected Witnesses (14:1)
III. The Perspective of the Lamb (14:2)
  A. The Voice from Heaven—Attesting to His Authority
  B. The Voice of Many Waters—Affirming His

name written in their fore-heads.

2 And I heard a voice from heaven, as the voice of many waters, and as the voice of a great thunder: and I heard the voice of harpers harping with their harps:

3 And they sung as it were a new song before the throne, and before the four beasts, and the elders: and no man could learn that song but the hundred *and* forty *and* four thousand, which were re-deemed from the earth.

4 These are they which were not defiled with women; for they are virgins. These are they which follow the Lamb whithersoever he goeth. These were redeemed from among men, *being* the firstfruits unto God and to the Lamb.

5 And in their mouth was found no guile: for they are without fault before the throne of God.

6 ¶And I saw another angel fly in the midst of heaven, hav-ing the everlasting gospel to preach unto them that dwell on the earth, and to every na-tion, and kindred, and

The
New Song
of the
144,000

Power
    C.   The Voices of Harpers—Asserting His Worship
        1. Their Harps—a Symbol of their Concord
        2. Their Song—a Symbol of their Conquest
IV.   The New Song of the 144,000 (14:3-5)
    A.   As a Testimony to the Lamb's Refuge
        1. Before the Throne—Directed toward God
        2. Before the Beasts—Directed to the Angels
        3. Before the Elders—Directed to the Church
    B.   As a Testimony of the Lamb's Redemption
        1. Unable to Be Learned by Others—God's Special Promise to the Elect…Atonement
        2. Unique in its Application—God's Special Provision to the Elect… Restoration
    C.   As a Testimony of the Elects' Resolve
        1. Their Flawless Reputation—Purity in Life
        2. Their Faithful Resolution—Purpose of Life
        3. Their Factual Redemption—Propitiation to New Life
        4. Their Fruitful Reproduction—Propagation of Life Everlasting
        5. Their Faultless Respect—Proper Living
V.   The First Messenger—Proclamation of the Gospel
    A.   The Participant—By the Flying Angel
    B.   The Placement—In the Midst of Heaven
    C.   The Preaching—To Those on Earth
    D.   The Proclamation—Judgment
        1. Fear of God—Respect His Authority
        2. Glorify God—Recognize His Majesty
        3. Judgment is Come—Reckon His Justice
        4. Worship the Creator—Realize His Design

tongue, and people,

7 Saying with a loud voice, Fear God, and give glory to him; for the hour of his judgment is come: and worship him that made heaven, and earth, and the sea, and the fountains of waters.

8 And there followed another angel, saying, Babylon is fallen, is fallen, that great city, because she made all nations drink of the wine of the wrath of her fornication.

9 And the third angel followed them, saying with a loud voice, If any man worship the beast and his image, and receive *his* mark in his forehead, or in his hand,

10 The same shall drink of the wine of the wrath of God, which is poured out without mixture into the cup of his indignation; and he shall be tormented with fire and brimstone in the presence of the holy angels, and in the presence of the Lamb:

11 And the smoke of their torment ascendeth up for ever and ever: and they have no rest day nor night, who worship the beast and his image, and whosoever receiveth the

"Babylon is fallen, is fallen, that great city"

a) Over Man as his God
b) Over Man as his Go-Between
c) Over Man as his Genesis

Three messengers (angels) are introduced in this chapter. The first angel proclaims the Everlasting Gospel—a reminder of the good news of God's certain pardon; the second angel publishes the fall of Babylon—a reminder of God's swift punishment; the third angel pronounces judgment upon those who receive the mark of the Beast—a reminder of God's sure penalty. Their appearance falls after the new song of the 144,000 and just before the reaping of the full and bloody winepress by Jesus Christ, the Righteous Judge of the whole earth.

VI.   The Second Messenger—Publication of Babylon's Fall (14: 8)
    A.   The Simple Declaration—Judgment Has Come to the Disobedient
    B.   The Sure Discernment—Justice Has Been Served on the Defiant
       1. Her Duty to the Nations
       2. Her Defilement of the Nations
VII. The Third Messenger—Pronouncement of Judgment (14: 9-11)
    A.   The Men of Judgment
       1. Those who Worship the Beast and his Image
       2. Those who Receive the Mark of the Beast
    B.   The Measure of Judgment
       1. Without Mixture— Undiluted with Mercy
       2. With Indignation—Untempered by Grace
    C.   The Method of Judgment

mark of his name.

12 Here is the patience of the saints: here *are* they that keep the commandments of God, and the faith of Jesus.

13 ¶ And I heard a voice from heaven saying unto me, Write, Blessed *are* the dead which die in the Lord from henceforth: Yea, saith the Spirit, that they may rest from their labours; and their works do follow them.

14 And I looked, and behold a white cloud, and upon the cloud *one* sat like unto the Son of man, having on his head a golden crown, and in his hand a sharp sickle.

15 And another angel came out of the temple, crying with a loud voice to him that sat on the cloud, Thrust in thy sickle, and reap: for the time is come for thee to reap; for the harvest of the earth is ripe.

16 And he that sat on the cloud thrust in his sickle on the earth; and the earth was

The Presentation of the Son of Man

- His White Cloud—His Pure Majesty

- His Golden Crown—His Perfect Sovereignty

- His Sharp Sickle—His Powerful Judgment

   1. Without Relief—Tormented with Fire and Brimstone

   2. With Witnesses

    a) In the Presence of the Angels

    b) In the Presence of The Lamb

  D. The Mark of Judgment

   1. The Evidence of Their Judgment—the Smoke of their Torment Ascending up Forever

   2. The Excruciation of Their Judgment—No Rest Day or Night

   3. The Echo of Their Judgment

    a) Against Those who Worship the Beast and His Image

    b) Against Those who Receive the Mark of the Beast

VIII. The Patience of the Saints (14: 12)

  A. Their Obedience—Keeping the Commandments of God

  B. Their Orthodoxy—Keeping the Faith of Jesus

IX. The Proclamation of Blessing (14: 13)

  A. The Commendation from Above

   1. As to Authority

   2. As to Approval

  B. The Command to the Author

  C. The Confirmation of Agreement

   1. Affirmed by the Spirit

   2. Accepted in their Rest

   3. Attested to by their Works

X. The Presentation of the Son of Man (14:14)

  A. His White Cloud—His Pure Majesty

  B. His Golden Crown—His Perfect Sovereignty

  C. His Sharp Sickle—His Powerful Judgment

reaped.

17 And another angel came out of the temple which is in heaven, he also having a sharp sickle.

18 And another angel came out from the altar, which had power over fire; and cried with a loud cry to him that had the sharp sickle, saying, Thrust in thy sharp sickle, and gather the clusters of the vine of the earth; for her grapes are fully ripe.

19 And the angel thrust in his sickle into the earth, and gathered the vine of the earth, and cast *it* into the great winepress of the wrath of God.

20 And the winepress was trodden without the city, and blood came out of the winepress, even unto the horse bridles, by the space of a thousand *and* six hundred furlongs.

Unto the Horse Bridles

XI. The Pronouncement of the Angel (14: 15)
    A.   His Origin—out of the Temple
    B.   His Oration
        1. Crying—Denoting His Passion
        2. With a Loud Voice—Denoting His Power
        3. To Him that Sat on the Cloud—Denoting His Purpose
    C.   His Order
        1. Thrust in thy Sickle—the Swiftness of Judgment
        2. To Reap—the Sureness of Judgment
        3. Time is Come—the Season of Judgment
        4. The Harvest of the Earth is Ripe—the Sense of Judgment
XII. The Participants of Judgment (14: 16-19)
    A.   He That Sat on the Cloud
        1. His Designation—Authority in Judgment
        2. His Duty—Thrusting the Sickle
        3. His Direction—To the Earth
    B.   Another Angel Out of the Heavenly Temple
        1. His Designation—Agreement from the Father
        2. His Duty—Bearing another Sharp Sickle
        3. His Direction—To the Earth
    C.   Another Angel Out from the Altar
        1. His Designation—Assurance before the Persecuted
        2. His Duty
           a) Power Over Fire
           b) Proclaiming Judgment
              (1) Thrust in Thy Sharp Sickle—The Gravity of Judgment
              (2)   Gather the Vine of the Earth—The

Chapter 15

1 ¶ And I saw another sign in heaven, great and marvellous, seven angels having the seven last plagues; for in them is filled up the wrath of God.

2 And I saw as it were a sea of glass mingled with fire: and them that had gotten the victory over the beast, and over his image, and over his mark, *and* over the number of his name, stand on the sea of glass, having the harps of God.

3 And they sing the song of Moses the servant of God, and the song of the Lamb, saying, Great and marvellous *are* thy works, Lord God Almighty; just and true *are* thy ways, thou King of saints.

4 Who shall not fear thee, O Lord, and glorify thy name? for *thou* only *art* holy: for all nations shall come and worship before thee; for thy judgments are made manifest.

κυριε ο θεος ο παντοκρατωρ

Lord God Almighty

114

Goal of Judgment

(3) Grapes are Fully Ripe—The Growth to Judgment

D. The Performance of Their Duty (14: 20)
1. The Gleaning with the Sickle
2. The Gathering of the Vine
3. The Great Winepress of the Wrath of God
   a) Trodden without the City
   b) Pressed out in Blood
   c) To the Horse's Bridle
   d) For 180+ miles

The Things Hereafter
Chapter 15

I. The Introduction of the Seven Last Plagues (15:1)
A. Its Manifestation—Great and Marvelous
B. Its Messengers—Seven Angels
1. Significant because of their Participation
2. Significant because of their Number—7 being the number of Completion
C. Its Makeup—The Seven Last Plagues

II. The Image of the Sea of Glass (15:2-4)
A. The Sea Itself
1. A Sea—Indicative of Proportion
2. Of Glass—Indicative of Purity
3. Mingled with Fire—Indicative of Passage
B. The Sea's Inhabitants
1. Victors Over The Beast—Overcoming his Supremacy
2. Victors Over The Image—Overcoming his System
3. Victors Over the Mark—Overcoming his Symbol
C. The Singers' Song

5 ¶ And after that I looked, and, behold, the temple of the tabernacle of the testimony in heaven was opened:

6 And the seven angels came out of the temple, having the seven plagues, clothed in pure and white linen, and having their breasts girded with golden girdles.

7 And one of the four beasts gave unto the seven angels seven golden vials full of the wrath of God, who liveth for ever and ever.

8 And the temple was filled with smoke from the glory of God, and from his power; and no man was able to enter into the temple, till the seven plagues of the seven angels were fulfilled.

Moses' Song of Deliverance

1 ¶ Then sang Moses and the children of Israel this song unto the LORD, and spake, saying, I will sing unto the LORD, for he hath triumphed gloriously: the horse and his rider hath he thrown into the sea.

2 The LORD is my strength and song, and he is become my salvation: he is my God, and I will prepare him an habitation; my father's God, and I will exalt him.

3 The LORD is a man of war: the LORD is his name.

4 Pharaoh's chariots and his host hath he cast into the sea: his chosen captains also are drowned in the Red sea.

5 The depths have covered them: they sank into the bottom as a stone.

6 Thy right hand, O LORD, is become glorious in power: thy right hand, O LORD, hath dashed in pieces the enemy.

7 And in the greatness of thine excellency thou hast overthrown them that rose up against thee: thou sentest forth thy wrath, which consumed them as stubble.

8 And with the blast of thy nostrils the waters were gathered together, the floods stood upright as an heap, and the depths were congealed in the heart of the sea.

9 The enemy said, I will pursue, I will overtake, I will divide the spoil; my lust shall be satisfied upon them; I will draw my sword, my hand shall destroy them.

10 Thou didst blow with thy wind, the sea covered them: they sank as lead in the mighty waters.

11 Who is like unto thee, O LORD, among the gods? who is like thee, glorious in holiness, fearful in praises, doing wonders?

12 Thou stretchedst out thy right hand, the earth swallowed them.

13 Thou in thy mercy hast led forth the people which thou hast redeemed: thou hast guided them in thy strength unto thy holy habitation.

14 The people shall hear, and be afraid: sorrow shall take hold on the inhabitants of Palestina.

15 Then the dukes of Edom shall be amazed; the mighty men of Moab, trembling shall take hold upon them; all the inhabitants of Canaan shall melt away.

16 Fear and dread shall fall upon them; by the greatness of thine arm they shall be as still as a stone; till thy people pass over, O LORD, till the people pass over, which thou hast purchased.

17 Thou shalt bring them in, and plant them in the mountain of thine inheritance, in the place, O LORD, which thou hast made for thee to dwell in, in the Sanctuary, O Lord, which thy hands have established.

18 The LORD shall reign for ever and ever.

19 For the horse of Pharaoh went in with his chariots and with his horsemen into the sea, and the LORD brought again the waters of the sea upon them; but the children of Israel went on dry land in the midst of the sea.

1. The Song of Deliverance—Moses' Song (Compare Exodus 15:1-19)
2. The Song of Delight—The Song of the Lamb
   a) To His Ability—great and marvelous are thy works
   b) To His Authority—Lord God Almighty
   c) To His Attributes—just and true
   d) To His Autonomy—King of Saints
   e) To His Awesomeness
      (1) The Might of the Lord
      (2) The Majesty of His Name
      (3) The Magnificence of His Character
      (4) The Magnitude of His Worship
      (5) The Manifestation of His Judgments

III. The Indication of the Temple of the Tabernacle of the Testimony (15: 5-8)
   A. The Appearance of the Angels
      1. Their Origin—Out of the Temple
      2. Their Ordinal—Seven, the Sign of Fulfillment
      3. Their Office—Having the Seven Last Plagues
      4. Their Outfit
         a) Pure and White Linen—Symbol of their Holy Direction
         b) Golden Girdles—Symbol of their Righteous Protection
      5. Their Orders
         a) Their Proper Authority— Presented by one of the Four Beasts
         b) Their Powerful Armament—The Seven Vial Judgments

Chapter 16

1 ¶ And I heard a great voice out of the temple saying to the seven angels, Go your ways, and pour out the vials of the wrath of God upon the earth.

2 And the first went, and poured out his vial upon the earth; and there fell a noisome and grievous sore upon the men which had the mark of the beast, and *upon* them which worshipped his image.

The Seventh Seal
(The 7 Vial Judgments)

- *Vial 1:* Grievous sore against those who had received the mark of the Beast

- *Vial 2:* Sea turns to blood resulting in the death of all marine life

- *Vial 3:* Rivers and fresh waters become blood

- *Vial 4:* Sun scorches men with fire

- *Vial 5:* Darkness fills the Beast's kingdom

- *Vial 6:* River Euphrates is dried up to prepare for the Eastern invasion of the great two hundred million man army, leading to Armageddon

- *Vial 7:* The atmosphere is filled with the culminating judgment of God's wrath in conjunction with great hailstones of destruction

          (1) The Character of the Vials—Golden, Pure and Righteous

          (2) The Completeness of the Vials— Full of the Wrath of God

  B.   The Actions in the Temple

     1. The Revelation of the Power of God— revealed in smoke filling the Temple (see Isaiah 6:1-4; Exodus 40:34-35)

       a) Glory

       b) Power

     2. The Restriction of the Temple

       a) No man could enter until

       b) The seven plagues are completed

The Things Hereafter
Chapter 16

I.   The Voice of Authority (16:1)

  A.   The Source of the Great Voice—out of the Temple, Ordained by God Himself

  B.   The System of the Great Voice—go your ways, Ordered in an Orderly Manner

  C.   The Scope of the Great Command

     1. The Dimension of the Command—Pour out the vials of the wrath of God, the Indictment of God's Judgment

     2. The Direction of the Command—upon the earth, the Implementation of God's Judgment

II.   The Vials of Judgment (16: 2-21)

  A.   The First Vial

     1. Its Territory—the Earth

     2. Its Targets

       a) Against those who had the mark of the

3 And the second angel poured out his vial upon the sea; and it became as the blood of a dead *man*: and every living soul died in the sea.

4 And the third angel poured out his vial upon the rivers and fountains of waters; and they became blood.

5 And I heard the angel of the waters say, Thou art righteous, O Lord, which art, and wast, and shalt be, because thou hast judged thus.

6 For they have shed the blood of saints and prophets, and thou hast given them blood to drink; for they are worthy.

7 And I heard another out of the altar say, Even so, Lord God Almighty, true and righteous *are* thy judgments.

True and righteous are the judgments

        beast

      b) Against those who worshipped the beast

    3. Its Terrors

      a) Noisome Sore

      b) Grievous Sore

B.   The Second Vial

    1. Its Territory—the Sea

    2. Its Target—all living things in the sea

    3. Its Terror—the sea becomes as the blood of a dead man

C.   The Third Vial

    1. Its Territory—the Rivers and Fountains of Waters

    2. Its Terror—the waters become blood

    3. The Testimony of the Angel

      a) The Righteous God

        (1) His Eternality

          (a) Which art—His Ever Physical Existence

          (b) And wast—His Ever Present Existence

          (c) And shalt be—His Ever Promised Existence

        (2) His Execution—Righteous because He judges

      b) The Riotous People

        (1) Guilty of the Blood of the Saints

        (2) Guilty of the Blood of the Prophets

        (3) Given Blood to Drink

        (4) Good for Punishment; i.e., worthy

    4. The Testimony from the Altar—the Place of Martyrs

8 ¶ And the fourth angel poured out his vial upon the sun; and power was given unto him to scorch men with fire.

9 And men were scorched with great heat, and blasphemed the name of God, which hath power over these plagues: and they repented not to give him glory.

10 And the fifth angel poured out his vial upon the seat of the beast; and his kingdom was full of darkness; and they gnawed their tongues for pain,

The Kingdom of Darkness

a) Agreement Because of His Penalization

b) Agreement Because of His Power

c) Agreement Because of His Person

D. The Fourth Vial

1. Its Territory—the Sun

2. Its Target—the inhabitants of the earth

3. Its Terror

a) Scorching men with fire

b) Scorching men with great heat

4. Their Treachery

a) Against His Supremacy—Blaspheming the Name of God

b) Against His Sovereignty—which hath power over these plagues

c) Against His System—in not repenting according to God's plan

d) Against His Sanctity—in not giving God the Glory

E. The Fifth Vial

1. Its Territory—the Seat of the Beast, his capital

2. Its Target—the kingdom of the Beast

3. Its Terror

a) Filling the kingdom of the Beast with darkness—symbolic of Rejection of the True Light

b) Forcing the gnawing of their tongues—symbolic of their Repudiation of the True Light

c) Festering sores and pains—symbolic of their Reprobation because of their Rejection of the True Light

4. Their Response

11　And blasphemed the God of heaven because of their pains and their sores, and repented not of their deeds.

12 ¶ And the sixth angel poured out his vial upon the great river Euphrates; and the water thereof was dried up, that the way of the kings of the east might be prepared.

13　And I saw three unclean spirits like frogs *come* out of the mouth of the dragon, and out of the mouth of the beast, and out of the mouth of the false prophet.

14　For they are the spirits of devils, working miracles, *which* go forth unto the kings of the earth and of the whole world, to gather them to the battle of that great day of God Almighty.

15　Behold, I come as a thief. Blessed *is* he that watcheth, and keepeth his garments, lest he walk naked, and they see his shame.

16　And he gathered them together into a place called in the Hebrew tongue Armageddon.

17 ¶ And the seventh angel poured out his vial into the air; and there came a great

αρμαγεδδων

Armageddon

          a) Against His Deity—Blasphemy against the God of Heaven

          b) Against His Dictates—refusing to repent

          c) Against His Deeds—choosing their deeds over His Deed, i.e., His Gift

F.   The Sixth Vial

   1. Its Territory—the great river Euphrates

   2. Its Target

      a) To dry up its waters

      b) To allow the Kings of the East (the Oriental army of 200,000,000 soldiers) to pass over on dry ground

   3. Its Terror—Three Unclean Frog-like spirits

      a) Their Source

         (1) From the mouth of the dragon—the Lies of a False God

         (2) From the mouth of the beast—the Lies of a False Government

         (3) From the mouth of the false prophet—the Lies of a False Religion

      b) Their Service

         (1) Propaganda—Lying spirits working miracles

         (2) Propagation—to the kings of the earth and the whole world

         (3) Preparation—gather a lost world to judgment

   4. A Warning—He (Christ) comes as a Thief

   5. A Watch—Be Determined

      a) Keep the Garments—Be Diligent

      b) Lest they walk in their nakedness and

voice out of the temple of heaven, from the throne, saying, It is done.

18 And there were voices, and thunders, and lightnings; and there was a great earthquake, such as was not since men were upon the earth, so mighty an earthquake, *and* so great.

19 And the great city was divided into three parts, and the cities of the nations fell: and great Babylon came in remembrance before God, to give unto her the cup of the wine of the fierceness of his wrath.

20 And every island fled away, and the mountains were not found.

21 And there fell upon men a great hail out of heaven, *every stone* about the weight of a talent: and men blasphemed God because of the plague of the hail; for the plague thereof was exceeding great.

Chapter 17

1 ¶ And there came one of the seven angels which had the seven vials, and talked with

be ashamed

      6. The Result—God gathers a rebellious world to Armageddon

G.   The Seventh Vial

      1. Its Territory—the Air

      2. Its Target—to Deliver the Divine Message… "It is done"

      3. Its Terror (See Exodus 20:18)

        a) Voices

        b) Thunders

        c) Lightnings

        d) Great Earthquake

          (1) Its Extent—"such as was not since men were on the earth"

          (2) Its Effect

            (a) Jerusalem divided in three parts—"the great city"

            (b) Cities of the Nations Fall

            (c) Babylon given the "cup of the wine of the fierceness of God's wrath"

            (d) The Islands are destroyed

            (e) The Mountains are leveled

            (f) Great Hailstones fall upon men

            (g) Men blaspheme God for their calamities

Chapter 17 illustrates Satan's imitation of God's perfect order.

The Things Hereafter
Chapter 17

I.   The Exposition of the Judgment of the Great Whore (17: 1-6)

    A.   The Extent of Her Sin

me, saying unto me, Come hither; I will shew unto thee the judgment of the great whore that sitteth upon many waters:

2 With whom the kings of the earth have committed fornication, and the inhabitants of the earth have been made drunk with the wine of her fornication.

3 So he carried me away in the spirit into the wilderness: and I saw a woman sit upon a scarlet coloured beast, full of names of blasphemy, having seven heads and ten horns.

4 And the woman was arrayed in purple and scarlet colour, and decked with gold and precious stones and pearls, having a golden cup in her hand full of abominations and filthiness of her fornication:

5 And upon her forehead *was* a name written, MYSTERY, BABYLON THE GREAT, THE MOTHER OF HAR- LOTS AND ABOMINA- TIONS OF THE EARTH.

6 And I saw the woman drunken with the blood of the saints, and with the

THE WOMAN'S NAME

- MYSTERY

- BABYLON THE GREAT

- THE MOTHER OF HAR- LOTS

- AND ABOMINATIONS OF THE EARTH

WRITTEN UPON HER

FOREHEAD

1. The Scope of Her Outreach—sitting upon many waters
2. The Source of Her Order—committing fornication with the kings of the earth
3. The Scheme of Her Organization—make the inhabitants of the earth drunk with the wine of her fornication

B. The Expression of Her Appearance
1. A Woman—Her Attributes Sitting—Her Alliance
2. Upon a Scarlet Colored Beast—Her Association
3. Full of the Names of Blasphemy—Her Attitudes
4. Having Seven Heads—Her Authority
5. Having Ten Horns—Her Administration

C. The Exhibit of Her Adornment
1. Arrayed in Purple and Scarlet—the Blood of Martyrs
2. Decked with Gold—Betraying Deity
3. Precious Stones—Betraying Worthiness
4. Pearls—Betraying God's Handiwork
5. Holding a Golden Cup
   a) Full of Abominations
   b) Full of the Filthiness of Her Fornications

D. The Evidence of Her Autograph
1. Upon her Forehead—Attesting to her Lust for "science, falsely so-called"
2. MYSTERY—that which was once hidden now revealed
3. BABYLON THE GREAT—see Daniel 4:30

blood of the martyrs of Jesus: and when I saw her, I wondered with great admiration.

7 ¶ And the angel said unto me, Wherefore didst thou marvel? I will tell thee the mystery of the woman, and of the beast that carrieth her, which hath the seven heads and ten horns.

8 The beast that thou sawest was, and is not; and shall ascend out of the bottomless pit, and go into perdition: and they that dwell on the earth shall wonder, whose names were not written in the book of life from the foundation of the world, when they behold the beast that was, and is not, and yet is.

9 And here *is* the mind which hath wisdom. The seven heads are seven mountains, on which the woman sitteth.

10 And there are seven kings: five are fallen, and one is, *and* the other is not yet come; and when he cometh, he must continue a short space.

11 And the beast that was, and is not, even he is the eighth, and is of the seven, and goeth into perdition.

Mysteries Revealed

- The Woman

- The Beast

- The Seven Heads

- The Ten Horns

- The Waters

- The Will of God

12　And the ten horns which thou sawest are ten kings, which have received no kingdom as yet; but receive power as kings one hour with the beast.

13　These have one mind, and shall give their power and strength unto the beast.

14 ¶ These shall make war with the Lamb, and the Lamb shall overcome them: for he is Lord of lords, and King of kings: and they that are with him *are* called, and chosen, and faithful.

15　And he saith unto me, The waters which thou sawest, where the whore sitteth, are peoples, and multitudes, and nations, and tongues.

16　And the ten horns which thou sawest upon the beast, these shall hate the whore, and shall make her desolate and naked, and shall eat her flesh, and burn her with fire.

17　For God hath put in their hearts to fulfil his will, and to agree, and give their kingdom unto the beast, until the words of God shall be fulfilled.

18　And the woman which thou sawest is that great city,

The
Saints
of God

Called

Chosen

Faithful

Seven Mountains (Probably Kingdoms) and Seven Kings

    1. Five Kings are Fallen—Historical as of John's Time (See Daniel 2:31-45)

    2. One Is—Current as of John's Time…the Kingdom of Rome

    3. One Not Yet Come—Future as of John's Time…the Kingdom of the Anti-Christ

D.   The Mystery of the Ten Horns Revealed—Ten Kings

    1. A Future Alliance

    2. A Fixed Authority

    3. A Faulty Allegiance

E.   The Misguided Warfare with The Lamb

    1. Because the Lamb is Worthy

       a) He is Lord of Lords—Addressing His Sanctity

       b) He is King of Kings—Addressing His Sovereignty

    2. Because His Saints are Worthwhile

       a) They are Called

       b) They are Chosen

       c) They are Faithful

F.   The Mystery of the Waters Revealed

    1. Its Intimacy—Where the Whore Sits

    2. Its Identity

       a) Peoples

       b) Multitudes

       c) Nations

       d) Tongues

G.   The Mastery of God's Will Revealed

    1. The Disgust of the Whore

    2. The Desolation of the Whore

which reigneth over the kings of the earth.

Chapter 18

1 ¶ And after these things I saw another angel come down from heaven, having great power; and the earth was lightened with his glory.

2 And he cried mightily with a strong voice, saying, Babylon the great is fallen, is fallen, and is become the habitation of devils, and the hold of every foul spirit, and a cage of every unclean and hateful bird.

3 For all nations have drunk of the wine of the wrath of her fornication, and the kings of the earth have committed fornication with her, and the merchants of the earth are waxed rich through the abundance of her delicacies.

3. The Devouring of the Whore
4. The Desecration of the Whore
5. Their Destiny with the Whore
   a) To Fulfill God's Will—Attesting to His Continued Sovereignty
   b) To Forfeit their Governments—Attesting to their Convoluted Sense

The Things Hereafter
Chapter 18

I. The Appearance of the Mighty Angel (18:1)
  A. His Emergence—Come Down From Heaven
  B. His Efficacy—Having Great Power
  C. His Eminence—the Earth Lightened with his Glory

II. The Announcement of the Mighty Angel (18: 2-3)
  A. The Intensity of his Proclamation
    1. Mightily
    2. With a Strong Voice
  B. The Information of his Proclamation
    1. The Destruction of Babylon Announced—Babylon is fallen, is fallen
    2. The Desolation of Babylon is Acknowledged
      a) The habitation of devils
      b) The hold of every foul spirit
      c) The cage of every unclean and hateful bird
  C. The Indictment of his Proclamation
    1. Against the Nations
      a) Partakers of her Wine—the Intoxication of her Wealth
      b) Partakers of her Wrath—the Inheritance

4 And I heard another voice from heaven, saying, Come out of her, my people, that ye be not partakers of her sins, and that ye receive not of her plagues.

5 For her sins have reached unto heaven, and God hath remembered her iniquities.

6 Reward her even as she rewarded you, and double unto her double according to her works: in the cup which she hath filled fill to her double.

7 How much she hath glorified herself, and lived deliciously, so much torment and sorrow give her: for she saith in her heart, I sit a queen, and am no widow, and shall see no sorrow.

8 Therefore shall her plagues come in one day, death, and mourning, and famine; and she shall be utterly burned with fire: for strong *is* the Lord God who judgeth her.

Double Unto Her Double

of her Wickedness
- c) Partakers of her Waywardness—the Illicitness of her Wrong
2. Against the Kings—for Their Fornication with Her
3. Against the Merchants
- a) For Their Choice of Affluence over Right
- b) For Their Choice of Abundance over Righteousness

III. The Attestation of the Majestic Voice (18: 4-8)
- A. The Identity of the Second Voice
  1. Arising from Heaven
  2. Announcing a Father—"my people"
- B. The Instruction of the Second Voice
  1. Remove Yourself From Her
  2. Renounce Her Sins
  3. Receive Not Her Plagues
- C. The Intensity of the Sin Visited
  1. Its Extent—Reaching to Heaven
  2. Its Exposition—God has Remembered Her Iniquities
- D. The Indoctrination of the Second Voice
  1. Reward Her Evenly—Even As
  2. Reward Her Energetically—Double Her Deeds
  3. Reward Her Excessively—Filled Full
     - a) Her Idolatry—Self Glorification
     - b) Her Import—Lavish Living
     - c) Her Incorrect Assumptions
       - (1) "I sit a queen"—Her Lofty Self-View
       - (2) "I am no widow"—Her Lack of

9 ¶ And the kings of the earth, who have committed fornication and lived deliciously with her, shall bewail her, and lament for her, when they shall see the smoke of her burning,

10 Standing afar off for the fear of her torment, saying, Alas, alas, that great city Babylon, that mighty city! for in one hour is thy judgment come.

11 And the merchants of the earth shall weep and mourn over her; for no man buyeth their merchandise any more:

12 The merchandise of gold, and silver, and precious stones, and of pearls, and fine linen, and purple, and silk, and scarlet, and all thyine wood, and all manner vessels of ivory, and all manner vessels of most precious wood, and of brass, and iron, and marble,

13 And cinnamon, and odours, and ointments, and frankincense, and wine, and oil, and fine flour, and wheat, and beasts, and sheep, and horses, and chariots, and slaves, and souls of men.

14 And the fruits that thy soul lusted after are departed

"in one hour is thy judgment come"

Piety

        d) "I shall see no sorrow"—Her Loss of Reality

E.   The Intent of the Sentence Made Visible

    1. Judgment By Plagues

        a) Their Fervor—In One Day

        b) Their Features

           (1) Death

           (2) Mourning

           (3) Famine

           (4) Fire

    2. Judgment That Is Proper

        a) By God's Might

        b) By God's Majesty

IV.   The Answer of the Mighty Men (18: 9-19)

A.   The Monarchs of the Earth—The Affiliation of the World's Governmental System

    1. Their Reputation

        a) Committed Fornication with Babylon

        b) Lived Deliciously with Babylon

    2. Their Reaction

        a) Bewailing the Destruction of Babylon

        b) Lamenting the Loss of Babylon's Wealth

    3. Their Response

        a) The Sorrow of the Judgment—Alas, Alas

        b) The Scope of the Judgment—Great City Babylon, That Mighty City

        c) The Swiftness of the Judgment—In One Hour

B.   The Merchants of the Earth—The Affiliation of the World's Economic System

from thee, and all things which were dainty and goodly are departed from thee, and thou shalt find them no more at all.

15 The merchants of these things, which were made rich by her, shall stand afar off for the fear of her torment, weeping and wailing,

16 And saying, Alas, alas, that great city, that was clothed in fine linen, and purple, and scarlet, and decked with gold, and precious stones, and pearls!

17 For in one hour so great riches is come to nought. And every shipmaster, and all the company in ships, and sailors, and as many as trade by sea, stood afar off,

18 And cried when they saw the smoke of her burning, saying, What *city is* like unto this great city!

19 And they cast dust on their heads, and cried, weeping and wailing, saying, Alas, alas, that great city, wherein were made rich all that had ships in the sea by reason of her costliness! for in one hour is she made desolate.

Alas, Alas That Great City

1. Their Reputation
    a) Their Trade in the Stores of Merchandise
    b) Their Trade in the Souls of Men
    c) Their Trade in the Specialties of Men's Lusts
2. Their Reaction
    a) They Shall Weep and Mourn at the Loss of Their Trade
    b) They Shall Weep and Wail out of the Fear of Her Torment
3. Their Response
    a) The Sorrow of the Judgment—Alas, Alas
    b) The Scope of the Judgment
        (1) Babylon's Opulent Past
        (2) Babylon's Overwhelming Punishment
    c) The Swiftness of the Judgment—In One Hour

C. The Mariners of the Earth—The Affiliation of the World's Transportation System
    1. Their Reputation
        a) The Extent of Their Corruption
            (1) Every Shipmaster
            (2) All the Company
            (3) As Many as Trade
        b) The Excesses of Their Corruption—Made Rich...by Reason of Her Costliness
    2. Their Reaction
        a) Their Dread—Standing Afar Off
        b) Their Dirge—Seeing the Smoke of Her

20   Rejoice over her, *thou* heaven, and *ye* holy apostles and prophets; for God hath avenged you on her.

21   And a mighty angel took up a stone like a great millstone, and cast *it* into the sea, saying, Thus with violence shall that great city Babylon be thrown down, and shall be found no more at all.

22   And the voice of harpers, and musicians, and of pipers, and trumpeters, shall be heard no more at all in thee; and no craftsman, of whatsoever craft *he be*, shall be found any more in thee; and the sound of a millstone shall be heard no more at all in thee;

23   And the light of a candle shall shine no more at all in thee; and the voice of the bridegroom and of the bride shall be heard no more at all in thee: for thy merchants were the great men of the earth; for by thy sorceries were all nations deceived.

24   And in her was found the blood of prophets, and of saints, and of all that were slain upon the earth.

The Blood of Prophets

Burning

      c) Their Disgrace—Sackcloth

    3. Their Response

      a) The Sorrow of the Judgment—Alas, Alas

      b) The Scope of the Judgment—That Great City, from Riches to Desolation

      c) The Swiftness of the Judgment—In One Hour

V.   The Avenged Saints Response (18: 20)

   A.   The Hosts of Heaven Rejoice

   B.   The Holy Apostles Rejoice

   C.   The Honored Prophets Rejoice

VI.   The Act of the Mighty Angel (18: 21-23)

   A.   The Gathering of Great Millstone—Symbolic of the Cataclysmic Judgment of God

   B.   The Casting it into the Sea—Symbolic of the Comprehensive Judgment of God

   C.   The Explanation of the Mighty Act

    1. Defined by violence

    2. Delineated by defeat

    3. Distinguished by utter destruction

      a) Desolation of the Composers

        (1) No Harpers

        (2) No Musicians

        (3) No Pipers

        (4) No Trumpeters

      b) Desecration of the Craftsmen

      c) Destruction of the Commerce—the Sound of the Millstone shall be heard no more

      d) Devastation of the Community

        (1) Collapse of Normal Services

Chapter 19

1 ¶ And after these things I heard a great voice of much people in heaven, saying, Alleluia; Salvation, and glory, and honour, and power, unto the Lord our God:

2 For true and righteous *are* his judgments: for he hath judged the great whore, which did corrupt the earth with her fornication, and hath avenged the blood of his servants at her hand.

ALLELUIA SALVATION GLORY HONOUR AND POWER

    (2) Cessation of Nuptial Services
   4. Determined by Disobedience
    a) The Deception of the Sorceries—
     φαρμακεια, the distribution of drugs
    b) The Death of the Sacrificed Martyrs
     (1) Blood of the Seers
     (2) Blood of the Saints
     (3) Blood of the Slain

The Things Hereafter

Chapter 19

I. The Aftermath of the Fall of Babylon—the Heavenly Viewpoint (19:1-4)
 A. What Was Heard
   1. A Great Voice—the Singularity of the Agreement
   2. Of Much People—the Scope of the Assemblage
   3. In Heaven—The Site of the Assembly
 B. What Was Said
   1. Alleluia—Praise to Jehovah, the Direction of the Statement
   2. Attributes— Properties of Jehovah
    a) Salvation—His Establishment of Our Relationship to Him
    b) Glory—His Expression of His Dignity Towards Us
    c) Honour—His Esteem in the Highest Degree
    d) Power—His Exhibition of Might to Us
    e) Unto the Lord our God—The Only Object of Our Affection
   3. Assessments—Principles of Jehovah
    a) His Judgments are Praised

3 And again they said, Alleluia. And her smoke rose up for ever and ever.

4 And the four and twenty elders and the four beasts fell down and worshipped God that sat on the throne, saying, Amen; Alleluia.

Amen

&

Alleluia

(1) True

(2) Righteous

b) His Judgments are Purposed—He has Judged the Great Whore

(1) Because she corrupted the earth with her fornication

(2) Because of the innocents' blood that was shed by her hand

C. What Was Said Again—Alleluia, Praise to Jehovah

D. What Was Seen—The Utter Destruction of Babylon

1. The Smoke—Depicting The Residue Following the Judgment of God

2. Its Rising—Depicting the Revelation of the Judgment of God

3. For Ever and Ever—Depicting the Relentlessness of the Judgment of God

E. What Was Done

1. Twenty Four Elders Fall Down—Symbolic of the Submission of the Redeemed

a) Worshipped God

(1) Because of His Sovereignty—His Position on the Throne

(2) Because of His Severity—His Punishment against Babylon

(3) Because of Their Agreement—Amen

(4) Because of His Deserved Praise—Alleluia

2. Four Beasts Fall Down—Symbolic of the Submission of the Angelic Host

(1)   Because of His Sovereignty—

5 ¶ And a voice came out of the throne, saying, Praise our God, all ye his servants, and ye that fear him, both small and great.

6 And I heard as it were the voice of a great multitude, and as the voice of many waters, and as the voice of mighty thunderings, saying, Alleluia: for the Lord God omnipotent reigneth.

7 Let us be glad and rejoice, and give honour to him: for the marriage of the Lamb is come, and his wife hath made herself ready.

The Voice of

A Great Multitude

Many Waters

Mighty Thunderings

PRAISE TO OUR GOD

- *The Directive of Praise*

- *The Duty of Praise*

- *The Design of Praise*

- *The Dominion of Praise*

Position on the Throne

(2) Because of His Severity—His Punishment against Babylon

(3) Because of Their Agreement—Amen

(4) Because of His Deserved Praise—Alleluia

II. The Affirmation of the Fall of Babylon—The Heavenly Voice (19: 5-10)

    A. The Voice Determined

        1. His Domain—Out of the Throne

        2. His Decree

            a) Praise to Our God—The Directive of Praise

            b) All His Servants—The Duty of Praise

            c) All Who Fear Him—The Design of Praise

            d) Both Small and Great—the Dominion of Praise

    B. The Voice Described—As It Were

        1. The Voice of a Great Multitude—The All Surrounding Aspect of His Character

        2. The Voice of Many Waters—The All Sustaining Aspect of His Character

        3. The Voice of Mighty Thunderings—The All Sturdy Aspect of His Character

    C. The Voice Declared

        1. Alleluia—Praise to Jehovah, Praise to God Approved

        2. Authority—Domain of the Lord God

            a) Omnipotence

            b) Sovereignty

        3. Announcement—The Marriage of the

8 And to her was granted that she should be arrayed in fine linen, clean and white: for the fine linen is the righteousness of saints.

9 And he saith unto me, Write, Blessed *are* they which are called unto the marriage supper of the Lamb. And he saith unto me, These are the true sayings of God.

10 And I fell at his feet to worship him. And he said unto me, See *thou do it* not: I am thy fellowservant, and of thy brethren that have the testimony of Jesus: worship God: for the testimony of Jesus is the spirit of prophecy.

11 ¶ And I saw heaven opened, and behold a white horse; and he that sat upon him *was* called Faithful and True, and in righteousness he doth judge and make war.

12 His eyes *were* as a flame of fire, and on his head *were* many crowns; and he had a name written, that no man knew, but he himself.

Lamb is Come
- a) Reaction of the Saints—Be Glad and Rejoice
- b) Reward of the Saved—Give Honor unto Him
- c) Readiness of the Spouse—the Wife has Made Herself Ready; the Bride is the Church
  - (1) Her Attire is Granted—Speaks to Her Imputed Salvation
  - (2) Her Array is Fine Linen
    - (a) Clean—The Unsullied Glory of His Imputed Righteousness
    - (b) White—The Unspoiled Reflection of His Imputed Righteousness
  - (3) Her Attendants are Blessed
  - (4) Her Affirmation is Announced

D. The Veneration Misplaced
1. Reverence is For God's Glorification—not Man's, Worship God
2. Revelation is For God's Glory—not Man's, the Testimony of Jesus is the Spirit of Prophecy

III. The Appearance of the Son of God—The Heavenly Vicar (19:11-16)

A. His Mode of Transportation—A White Horse

B. His Mark of Recognition
1. He is Seated upon the White Horse—Symbolic of His Perfect Power
2. His Names
   - a) Faithful—Underlying His Character—Perfection

13 And he *was* clothed with a vesture dipped in blood: and his name is called The Word of God.

14 And the armies *which were* in heaven followed him upon white horses, clothed in fine linen, white and clean.

15 And out of his mouth goeth a sharp sword, that with it he should smite the nations: and he shall rule them with a rod of iron: and he treadeth the winepress of the fierceness and wrath of Almighty God.

16 And he hath on *his* vesture and on his thigh a name written, KING OF KINGS, AND LORD OF LORDS.

17 And I saw an angel standing in the sun; and he cried with a loud voice, saying to all the fowls that fly in the midst of heaven, Come and gather yourselves together unto the supper of the great God;

KING OF KINGS
and
LORD OF LORDS

b) True—Underpinning His Certainty—Purity

C.   His Means of Government
    1. Righteous Judgment
    2. Righteous Warfare

D.   His Manner of Description
    1. His Eyes—As a Flame of Fire, Symbolic of the Omnipresent Judgment of God
    2. On His Head—Many Crowns, Symbolic of the Omnipotence of God
    3. His Hidden Name—No Man Knew, but He Himself, Symbolic of the Omniscience of God
    4. His Clothing—a Vesture dipped in Blood, Symbolic of His All-Efficacious Atoning
    5. His Name Revealed—The Word of God, His All-Encompassing Authority
    6. His Armies
      a) Follow Him—Evidence of their Dedication
      b) Upon White Horses—Evidence of their Direction
      c) Clothed in White Linen—Evidence of their Distinction—His Righteousness
    7. His Mouth—Out of Which Goeth a Sharp Sword, Supporting His Righteous Sovereignty
      a) His Ferocity Against the Nations—The Smiting
      b) His Fortitude of His Own Sovereignty—Ruling With A Rod of Iron
      c) His Treading of the Winepress
        (1) Of the Fierceness of the Sovereign

18 That ye may eat the flesh of kings, and the flesh of captains, and the flesh of mighty men, and the flesh of horses, and of them that sit on them, and the flesh of all *men, both* free and bond, both small and great.

19 And I saw the beast, and the kings of the earth, and their armies, gathered together to make war against him that sat on the horse, and against his army.

20 And the beast was taken, and with him the false prophet that wrought miracles before him, with which he deceived them that had received the mark of the beast, and them that worshipped his image. These both were cast alive into a lake of fire burning with brimstone.

21 And the remnant were slain with the sword of him that sat upon the horse, which *sword* proceeded out of his mouth: and all the fowls were filled with their flesh.

Cast Alive into a Lake of Fire

God
(2) Of the Wrath of the Sovereign God
8. His Vesture and His Thigh, On It a Name
   a) KING OF KINGS, His Secular Authority
   b) AND LORD OF LORDS, His Spiritual Authority

IV. The Angel Standing in the Sun (19:17-18)
   A. His Audience—The Fowls that Fly in the Midst of Heaven
   B. His Announcement
     1. Come to the Place Appointed
     2. Gather to the Plate of God's Allocation, To Eat
       a) The Flesh of Kings
       b) The Flesh of Captains
       c) The Flesh of Mighty Men
       d) The Flesh of Horses
       e) The Flesh of Riders
       f) The Flesh of Free Men
       g) The Flesh of Bond Men
       h) The Flesh of Small Men
       i) The Flesh of Great Men

V. The Armies of Opposition (19:19-21)
   A. Their Confederacy
     1. The Beast—The Supreme Commander
     2. The Kings of the Earth—The Seditious Coalition
     3. The Armies of the Earth—the Subversive Confederation
   B. Their Cause
     1. To Make War Against the Christ—He Who Sat upon the Horse

Chapter 20

1 ¶ And I saw an angel come down from heaven, having the key of the bottomless pit and a great chain in his hand.

2 And he laid hold on the dragon, that old serpent, which is the Devil, and Satan, and bound him a thousand years,

3 And cast him into the bottomless pit, and shut him up, and set a seal upon him, that he should deceive the nations no more, till the thousand years should be fulfilled: and after that he must be loosed a little season.

Bound for a Thousand Years

2. To Make War Against the Saints—His Army
C.   Their Conclusion
1. They Both are Captured
a) The Beast is Taken
b) The False Prophet is Taken
(1) Deceiver of Those Who Received the Mark of the Beast
(2) Deceiver of Those Who Worshipped The Image of the Beast
2. They Both are Cast Alive into the Lake of Fire—Burning With Fire And Brimstone
3. Their Allies are Slain with the Sword
a) The Sword of Him That Sits Upon the Horse—The Messiah of God
b) The Sword of Him That Proceeds Out of His Mouth—The Message of God
4. The Fowls are Filled With Their Flesh

The Things Hereafter
Chapter 20
After Jacob's Trouble (Chapters 20-22)

I.   The Foremost Angel Come Down From Heaven (20: 1-3)
A.   His Instruments
1. The Key of The Bottomless Pit
2. A Great Chain
B.   His Intent
1. He Lays Hold On The Dragon
a) Aka, That Old Serpent
b) Aka, the Devil
c) Aka, Satan
2. He Binds Satan for a Thousand Years

4 And I saw thrones, and they sat upon them, and judgment was given unto them: and *I saw* the souls of them that were beheaded for the witness of Jesus, and for the word of God, and which had not worshipped the beast, neither his image, neither had received *his* mark upon their foreheads, or in their hands; and they lived and reigned with Christ a thousand years.

5 But the rest of the dead lived not again until the thousand years were finished. This *is* the first resurrection.

6 Blessed and holy *is* he that hath part in the first resurrection: on such the second death hath no power, but they shall be priests of God and of Christ, and shall reign with him a thousand years.

Blessed and Holy

a) Cast into a Bottomless Pit

b) Shut Up

c) Set a Seal Upon Him

C. His Incentive

1. That Satan Should Deceive the Nations No More—his Subterfuge

2. Until the Thousand Years are Fulfilled—his Sentence

3. Until He Must Be Loosed a Little Season—his Second Opportunity

II. The First Resurrection (20:4-6)

A. The Reign of the Saints

1. Their Destined Thrones—a Witness of Their Authority

2. Their Decreed Judgment—a Witness of Their Discernment

3. Their Description

(1) The Beheaded Ones

(a) For the Witness of Jesus

(b) For the Word of God

(2) The Believers

(a) Who Worshipped Not the Beast

(b) Who Worshipped Not the Image of the Beast

(c) Who Received Not the Mark of the Beast

4. Their Destiny

a) To Live With Christ a Thousand Years

b) To Reign With Christ a Thousand Years

B. The Remainder of the Dead

1. Live Not at This Time

2. Left to a Future Resurrection

C. The Reward of the Saints

7 And when the thousand years are expired, Satan shall be loosed out of his prison,

8 And shall go out to deceive the nations which are in the four quarters of the earth, Gog and Magog, to gather them together to battle: the number of whom *is* as the sand of the sea.

9 And they went up on the breadth of the earth, and compassed the camp of the saints about, and the beloved city: and fire came down from God out of heaven, and devoured them.

10 And the devil that deceived them was cast into the lake of fire and brimstone, where the beast and the false prophet *are*, and shall be tormented day and night for ever and ever.

Tormented Day and Night

1. Blessed are Those Who Partake of the First Resurrection—Bespeaking the Satisfaction of the Believer
2. Holy are Those Who Partake of the First Resurrection—Bespeaking the Spirit of the Believer
3. Second Death is Powerless on Them—Bespeaking the Security of the Believer
4. They are Priests of God and Christ—Bespeaking the Status of the Believer
5. They Shall Reign with Christ for a Thousand Years—Bespeaking the Stability of the Believer

III. The Finish of the Thousand Years—The Millennium (20:7-10)

A. Satan Delivered Out of His Prison
B. Satan Deceives the Nations
1. The Scope of his Deception—the Four Quarters of the Earth, its Totality...the Whole World
2. The Spotlight of his Deception—Gog and Magog, its Totalitarianism...the Great Northern Confederacy (Russia, Germany, etc.)
3. The Scheme of his Deception—to Gather Them Together to Battle, its Theme...the Rebellious Coalition
4. The Scale of his Deception—as the Sand of the Sea, its Teeming...the Final Rebellion

C. Satan Directs the Nations Against the God of Eternity
1. Satan Directs his Armies Against

11 ¶ And I saw a great white throne, and him that sat on it, from whose face the earth and the heaven fled away; and there was found no place for them.

12 And I saw the dead, small and great, stand before God; and the books were opened: and another book was opened, which is *the book* of life: and the dead were judged out of those things which were written in the books, according to their works.

13 And the sea gave up the dead which were in it; and death and hell delivered up the dead which were in them: and they were judged every man according to their works.

14 And death and hell were cast into the lake of fire. This is the second death.

15 And whosoever was not found written in the book of life was cast into the lake of fire.

The

Second

Death

Jerusalem
    a) The Camp of the Saints
    b) The Beloved City
  2. God Delivers Fire from Heaven and Devours the Rebellious Armies of Satan
D.   Satan is Delivered to His Final Punishment
  1. Cast into the Lake of Fire and Brimstone
  2. Cast into Punishment with the Beast and False Prophet
  3. Cast into Eternal Damnation and Suffering

IV. The Final Judgment—the Great White Throne (20:11-15)
A.   The Judge—God Himself
  1. He Occupies a Just Throne—A Symbol of His Sovereignty
  2. He Overcomes All Things—A Symbol of His Supremacy
    a) At His Face the Earth Flees Away
    b) At His Face the Heaven Flees Away
B.   The Judged—Lost Mankind, Each Himself
  1. The Dead Stand Before God
    a) Small Men
    b) Great Men
    c) All Men
  2. The Books Are Opened
    a) The Book of Works—a Record of Lost Men's Works
    b) The Book of Life—a Record of Christ's Redeemed
  3. The Source of the Dead
    a) The Sea—Symbolic of the Range of His Judgment
    b) Death—Symbolic of the Relentlessness

Chapter 21

1 ¶ And I saw a new heaven and a new earth: for the first heaven and the first earth were passed away; and there was no more sea.

2 And I John saw the holy city, new Jerusalem, coming down from God out of heaven, prepared as a bride adorned for her husband.

3 And I heard a great voice out of heaven saying, Behold, the tabernacle of God *is* with men, and he will dwell with them, and they shall be his people, and God himself shall be with them, *and be* their God.

4 And God shall wipe away all tears from their eyes; and there shall be no more death, neither sorrow, nor crying, neither shall there be any more pain: for the former things are passed away.

5 And he that sat upon the throne said, Behold, I make all things new. And he said unto me, Write: for these words are true and faithful.

The Former Things are Passed Away

of His Judgment
c) Hell—Symbolic of the Reach of His Judgment
4. The Second Death
a) Death Cast Into the Lake of Fire
b) Hell Cast Into the Lake of Fire
c) Those Whose Names Were Not Found Written in the Lamb's Book of Life

The Things Hereafter

Chapter 21
After Jacob's Trouble (Chapters 20-22)

I. The Appearance of the New Heaven and the New Earth (21:1-5)
A. Things Which are Ended
1. The First Heaven Passes Away
2. The First Earth Passes Away
3. The Sea Ceases to exist
B. Things Which Are New
1. The New Royal City, Jerusalem—the Holy City
a) Its Designer—God
b) Its Descent—Out of Heaven
c) Its Description—Prepared as a Bride Adorned for her Husband
d) Its Decree—from the Great Voice
(1) The Presence of the Tabernacle with Men—the Scene of Worship
(2) The Presence of God with Men—the Source of Worship
(3) The Possession of Mankind as God's People—the Symbiotic Relationship of Worship

6   And he said unto me, It is done. I am Alpha and Omega, the beginning and the end. I will give unto him that is athirst of the fountain of the water of life freely.

7   He that overcometh shall inherit all things; and I will be his God, and he shall be my son.

8   But the fearful, and unbelieving, and the abominable, and murderers, and whoremongers, and sorcerers, and idolaters, and all liars, shall have their part in the lake which burneth with fire and brimstone: which is the second death.

CAST INTO THE

LAKE OF FIRE

- *Fearful*
- *Unbelieving*
- *Abominable*
- *Murderers*
- *Whoremongers*
- *Sorcerers*
- *Idolaters*
- *All Liars*

　　　　(4) The Personal Involvement of God with Men—the Sacred Nature of Worship

　　　　(5) The Particular Relationship of God with Men—the Special Aspect of Worship

　　2. The New Realm's Order

　　　a) No More Weeping—God shall wipe away all tears

　　　b) No More Death

　　　c) No More Sorrow nor Crying

　　　d) No More Pain

　　　e) No More Former Things

　　3. The New Promise is Made

　　　a) The Authority of the Promise—God, the Judge

　　　　(1) All Things Are Made Anew

　　　　(2) All Things Are Recorded

　　　b) The Assurance of the Promise

　　　　(1) True—Its Accuracy

　　　　(2) Faithful—Its Authenticity

II.　The Announcement of The Saviour (21:6-8)

　　A.　The Good News

　　　1. His Success—It is Done

　　　2. His Sufficiency

　　　　a) Alpha and Omega

　　　　b) Beginning and End

　　　3. His Satisfying

　　　　a) Its Focus—to him who is Athirst

　　　　b) Its Fulfillment

　　　　　(1) Fountain of the Water of Life—Abundance

　　　　　(2) Freely—Adequacy

9 ¶ And there came unto me one of the seven angels which had the seven vials full of the seven last plagues, and talked with me, saying, Come hither, I will shew thee the bride, the Lamb's wife.

10 And he carried me away in the spirit to a great and high mountain, and shewed me that great city, the holy Jerusalem, descending out of heaven from God,

11 Having the glory of God: and her light *was* like unto a stone most precious, even like a jasper stone, clear as crystal;

The Holy Jerusalem

4. His Stipulation—To him that over-cometh…an Inheritance of All Things—a Joint Heir
5. His Status
   a) I will be His Father
   b) He shall be My son
B.   The Bad News
   1. The Recipients of the Bad News
      a) The Fearful—Faithless
      b) The Unbelieving—Infidels
      c) The Abominable—literally "stinking", detestable
      d) The Murderers—Intentional Homicide
      e) The Whoremongers--Fornicators
      f) The Sorcerers—literally, relating to drugs
      g) The Idolaters—Image Worshippers
      h) The Liars—Deceivers
   2. The Results of the Bad News
      a) Their Portion—the Lake of Fire
      b) Their Position—the Second Death
III.   The Advent of the Holy Jerusalem (21: 9-27)
   A.   The Arrival of the Angel
      1. His Identity—One of the Seven Angels
      2. His Influence—Held a Vial Full of the Judgment of God
   B.   The Announcement of the Angel
      1. His Proclamation—Come Hither
      2. His Pronouncement—I Will Show Thee the Bride of the Lamb
   C.   The Activity of the Angel
      1. The Movement of John the Revelator
         a) The Direction—In the Spirit

12   And had a wall great and high, *and* had twelve gates, and at the gates twelve angels, and names written thereon, which are *the names* of the twelve tribes of the children of Israel:

13   On the east three gates; on the north three gates; on the south three gates; and on the west three gates.

14   And the wall of the city had twelve foundations, and in them the names of the twelve apostles of the Lamb.

15   And he that talked with me had a golden reed to measure the city, and the gates thereof, and the wall thereof.

16   And the city lieth foursquare, and the length is as large as the breadth: and he measured the city with the reed, twelve thousand furlongs. The length and the breadth and the height of it are equal.

17   And he measured the wall thereof, an hundred *and* forty *and* four cubits, *according to* the measure of a man, that is, of the angel.

18   And the building of the wall of it was *of* jasper: and the city *was* pure gold, like unto

4
SQUARE

b) The Destination—the Great and High Mountain

2. The Manifestation of the Great City—Holy Jerusalem

   a) Its Descent—Descending out of Heaven

   b) Its Designer—God Himself

   c) Its Demeanor—Having the Glory of God

   d) Its Deity—the Light of Christ's Presence

     (1) As Jasper (see Rev. 4:3 note)

     (2) As Clear as Crystal—denoting Perfection

D. The Attributes of the Holy City

1. Its Wall—Its Security

   a) Great—Its Vastness in the Presence of God

   b) High—Its Loftiness in the Economy of God

2. Its Gates—Its Accessibility

   a) Their Number—Twelve

   b) Their Keepers—Twelve Angels

   c) Their Namesakes—of the Twelve Tribes of Israel

   d) Their Location

     (1) East—Three Gates

     (2) North—Three Gates

     (3) South—Three Gates

     (4) West—Three Gates

3. Its Foundations

   a) Their Number—Twelve

   b) Their Namesakes—the Twelve Apostles

clear glass.

19 And the foundations of the wall of the city *were* garnished with all manner of precious stones. The first foundation *was* jasper; the second, sapphire; the third, a chalcedony; the fourth, an emerald;

20 The fifth, sardonyx; the sixth, sardius; the seventh, chrysolite; the eighth, beryl; the ninth, a topaz; the tenth, a chrysoprasus; the eleventh, a jacinth; the twelfth, an amethyst.

The Twelve Foundations

4. Its Measurements
   a) The Method of the Measurement—with a Perfect Measure, a Golden Reed
   b) The Measure of the City
      (1) Its Assessment, Foursquare—Indicative of its Perfection
      (2) Its Allocation, Twelve Thousand Furlongs (approximately 1500 miles)
   c) The Measure of the Wall
      (1) Its Assessment, by a Perfect Measure
      (2) Its Allocation, 144 Cubits (approximately 180-216 feet)
   d) The Masterpiece of the City
      (1) Purity—Wall of Jasper
      (2) Perfect Deity—City of Pure Gold, like unto clear glass
      (3) Precious Stones of the Foundation
         (a) First Foundation—Jasper, a White Stone (Purity) See Rev. 6:11; 7:9; 7:13
         (b) Second Foundation—Sapphire, a Blue Stone (Royalty) See Rev. 1:6; 5:10
         (c) Third Foundation—Chalcedony, a Copper-like Gem (Humanity) See Luke 9:58; 22:48
         (d) Fourth Foundation—Emerald, a Green Stone (Everlasting Goodness) See Psalm 73:1
         (e) Fifth Foundation—Sardonyx, a Banded Brown & White Stone

21 And the twelve gates *were* twelve pearls; every several gate was of one pearl: and the street of the city *was* pure gold, as it were transparent glass.

22 And I saw no temple therein: for the Lord God Almighty and the Lamb are the temple of it.

23 And the city had no need of the sun, neither of the moon, to shine in it: for the glory of God did lighten it, and the Lamb *is* the light thereof.

The Lamb is the Light Thereof

(Reminder of the Nature of Jesus Christ—100% man, 100% God) See Matt. 1:23; I Tim. 2:5

(f) Sixth Foundation— Sardius, a Red Stone (Christ's Blood) See Psalm 50:6

(g) Seventh Foundation—Chrysolite, a Golden Stone (Deity) See John 1:49

(h) Eighth Foundation—Beryl, a Colorless and Transparent Stone (Perfection) See II Sam. 22:31; Ps. 18:30

(i) Ninth Foundation—Topaz, a Hard & Colorless Stone in its Pure Form (Strength) See Isaiah 40:10

(j) Tenth Foundation — Chrysoprasus, a Greenish-Gold Stone (Enduring Mercy) See Ps. 45:6; 48:8; 52:8)

(k) Eleventh Foundation—Jacinth, a Blackish Red Stone, (Judgment) See Ps. 50:6; Ps. 67:4)

(l) Twelfth Foundation—Amethyst, a Purple Stone (Regal Piety & Sobriety) See Rev. 1:6; 5:10

(4) Perfection of the Construction

(a) Twelve Gates —made up of Twelve Singular Pearls (Preciousness of the True Church) See Eph. 5:25

(b) Transparent Golden Street

24 And the nations of them which are saved shall walk in the light of it: and the kings of the earth do bring their glory and honour into it.

25 And the gates of it shall not be shut at all by day: for there shall be no night there.

26 And they shall bring the glory and honour of the nations into it.

27 And there shall in no wise enter into it any thing that defileth, neither *whatsoever* worketh abomination, or *maketh* a lie: but they which are written in the Lamb's book of life.

The Lamb's Book of Life

(Purity of God's Handiwork) See Heb. 11:10

    (c) Temple—No Physical Temple Necessary

        (i) Lord God Almighty is the Temple (See Matt. 27:51)

        (ii) Lamb is the Temple (See Rom. 5:2; Eph. 2:18)

    (d) Totality of Light

        (i) Not by Natural Means

            (a) No Sun

            (b) No Moon

        (ii) Only by Supernatural Means

            (a) Glory of God Lights the City (See Isaiah 60:19)

            (b) Lamb is the Light of the City (See John 8:12; 9:5)

5. Its Activity

    a) The Realms who are Saved shall Walk in the Light

    b) The Rulers of the Earth shall Bring their Respect

        (1) They shall bring their Glory

        (2) They shall bring their Honor

    c) The Regularly Open Gates—Never Closed

    d) The Restricted from the City

        (1) Nothing Defiling

        (2) Nothing Detestable

        (3) Nothing Deceitful

    e) The Residents of the City—they who are written in the Lamb's Book of Life

Chapter 22

1 ¶ And he shewed me a pure river of water of life, clear as crystal, proceeding out of the throne of God and of the Lamb.

2 In the midst of the street of it, and on either side of the river, *was there* the tree of life, which bare twelve *manner of* fruits, *and* yielded her fruit every month: and the leaves of the tree *were* for the healing of the nations.

3 And there shall be no more curse: but the throne of God and of the Lamb shall be in it; and his servants shall serve him:

4 And they shall see his face; and his name *shall be* in their foreheads.

5 And there shall be no night there; and they need no candle, neither light of the sun; for the Lord God giveth them light: and they shall reign for ever and ever.

No More Curse

The Things Hereafter
Chapter 22
After Jacob's Trouble (Chapters 20-22)

I.   The Final Revelation of the Heavenly City (22: 1-5)
    A.   The River of the Water of Life
        1. Its Consistency—Clear as Glass
          a) Symbolic of its Life Giving Properties
          b) Symbolic of its Living Purity
        2. Its Course—Flowing from the Throne, symbolic of its Power
          a) Of God—Co-equal in Authority
          b) Of the Lamb—Co-equal in Power
    B.   The Tree of Life
        1. Its Place
          a) Midst of the Heavenly Street
          b) Either Side of the River of the Water of Life
        2. Its Produce
          a) Its Harvest—Monthly Yield
          b) Its Healing—Leaves for the Healing of the Nations
        3. The Throne of God and the Lamb
          a) No More Curse because of His Justice
          b) No Lack of Service Because of His Love to His Servants
          c) No Lack of Recognition
            (1) We Shall See Him Face to Face— Eternal Fellowship
            (2) We Shall Have His Name in Our Foreheads—Everlasting Possession
          d) No Need for Light Because of His Radiance

6 ¶ And he said unto me, These sayings *are* faithful and true: and the Lord God of the holy prophets sent his angel to shew unto his servants the things which must shortly be done.

7   Behold, I come quickly: blessed *is* he that keepeth the sayings of the prophecy of this book.

8 And I John saw these things, and heard *them*. And when I had heard and seen, I fell down to worship before the feet of the angel which shewed me these things.

9 Then saith he unto me, See *thou do it* not: for I am thy fellowservant, and of thy brethren the prophets, and of them which keep the sayings of this book: worship God.

10 And he saith unto me, Seal not the sayings of the prophecy of this book: for the time is at hand.

11 He that is unjust, let him be unjust still: and he which is filthy, let him be filthy still: and he that is righteous, let him be righteous still: and he that is holy, let him be holy still.

12 And, behold, I come quickly;

I
Come
Quickly

(1) No Night

(2) No Candle

(3) No Sun

(4) No End to Their Reign

II. The Final Reminder to the Revelator (22: 6-7)

    A. The Veracity of the Words of This Book—Sent by the God of the Prophets

    B. The Validity of the Words of This Book—Must Shortly Come to Pass

    C. The Vitality of the Words of This Book—Behold I Come Quickly

    D. The Verification of the Words of This Book—Blessing to Those who Keep the Words of This Prophecy

III. The Final Testimony of the Revelator (22: 8-11)

    A. The Personal Witness of the Events

        1. Things He had Seen

        2. Things He had Heard

    B. The Proper Worship after the Events

        1. Improper Direction—to the Angel

        2. Proper Direction—toward God

    C. The Particular Warning Regarding the Events

        1. Its Openness—Seal Not the Sayings of This Prophecy

        2. Its Urgency—the Time is at Hand

        3. Its Attitude

           a) Against the Unjust

           b) Against the Filthy

           c) For the Righteous

           d) For the Holy

IV. The Final Treatise of the Saviour (22: 12-19)

    A. The Circumstance of His Coming—Quickly

and my reward *is* with me, to give every man according as his work shall be.

13 I am Alpha and Omega, the beginning and the end, the first and the last.

14 Blessed *are* they that do his commandments, that they may have right to the tree of life, and may enter in through the gates into the city.

15 For without *are* dogs, and sorcerers, and whoremongers, and murderers, and idolaters, and whosoever loveth and maketh a lie.

16 I Jesus have sent mine angel to testify unto you these things in the churches. I am the root and the offspring of David, *and* the bright and morning star.

17 And the Spirit and the bride say, Come. And let him that heareth say, Come. And let him that is athirst come. And whosoever will, let him take the water of life freely.

AΩ

Alpha and Omega

B. The Compensation of His Coming
1. His Reward is with Him
2. His Reward is According to our Works
C. The Characteristics of His Character
1. Alpha and Omega
2. Beginning and End
3. First and Last
D. The Consent of His Coming
1. Blessings
a) Direction—to Those who Keep His Commandments
b) Rights to the Tree of Life
c) Entrance to the City
2. Curses
a) Direction—To Those who are Without
b) Description (See Rev. 21:8)
(1) Dogs
(2) Sorcerers
(3) Whoremongers
(4) Murders
(5) Idolaters
(6) Liars
E. The Confirmation of His Coming
1. The Testimony to the Churches
2. The Testimony of Jesus Christ
a) Root and Offspring of David, speaks as to His Rightful Authority
b) Bright and Morning Star, speaks as to His Radiant Attraction
3. The Testimony of the Spirit and the Bride
a) Come
b) Come, to Those who Hear
c) Come, to Those who Thirst

18 For I testify unto every man that heareth the words of the prophecy of this book, If any man shall add unto these things, God shall add unto him the plagues that are written in this book:

19 And if any man shall take away from the words of the book of this prophecy, God shall take away his part out of the book of life, and out of the holy city, and *from* the things which are written in this book.

20 ¶ He which testifieth these things saith, Surely I come quickly. Amen. Even so, come, Lord Jesus.

21 The grace of our Lord Jesus Christ *be* with you all. Amen.

Even so, come, Lord Jesus

        d) Conditional—Whosoever Will—
           Partake Freely

F.   The Caution of His Coming

    1. To Those Who Add to the Words of This Book—the Plagues of this Book Shall be Added to Them

    2. To Those Who Detract from the Words of This Book

       (1) God Shall Take Away His Part out of the Book of Life

       (2) God Shall Take Away His Part out of the Holy City

       (3) God Shall Take Away His Part of the Blessings of This Book

V.   The Final Postscript of the Book (22: 20-21)

    A.   The Certainty of His Coming—Surely

    B.   The Conciseness of His Coming—Quickly

    C.   The Consensus of His Coming

      1. Amen—So Let it Be

      2. Agreement—Even So, Come

    D.   The Conclusion of His Coming—the Grace of our Lord Jesus Christ be with you all. Amen

Amen